HEADLINE
WRITING

Sunil Saxena

SAGE Publications
New Delhi • Thousand Oaks • London

First published in 2006 by

Sage Publications India Pvt Ltd
B-42, Panchsheel Enclave
New Delhi 110 017
www.indiasage.com

Sage Publications Inc
2455 Teller Road
Thousand Oaks, California 91320

Sage Publications Ltd
1 Oliver's Yard, 55 City Road
London EC1Y 1SP

Published by Tejeshwar Singh for Sage Publications India Pvt. Ltd, phototypeset in 10.5/13 pt. Palatino at Excellent Laser Typesetters, Delhi, and printed at Chaman Enterprises, Delhi.

Library of Congress Cataloging-in-Publication Data

Saxena, Sunil.
    Headline writing / Sunil Saxena.
        p. cm.
    Includes index.
    1. Newspapers—Headlines. I. Title.

PN4784.H4S39   808'.06607—dc22   2006   2005033466

ISBN: 0–7619–3421–9 (PB)   81–7829–564–4 (India–PB)

Sage Production Team: Vineeta Rai, Jeevan Nair and Santosh Rawat

This book is dedicated to my mother
Shail Saxena

Contents

Foreword   9
Preface   11
Acknowledgements   13
List of Abbreviations   15

Chapter 1
Headline and its Functions   17

Chapter 2
How to Write a Headline   45

Chapter 3
Kinds of Headlines–I   58

Chapter 4
Kinds of Headlines–II   89

Chapter 5
Headline Props   119

Chapter 6
Feature and Magazine Headlines   138

Chapter 7
**Do's and Don'ts
The 25 Golden Rules**   169

Chapter 8
The Internet Headline   197

Glossary   205
Index   208
About the Author   210

Foreword

As a journalism teacher for some years now, I have frequently wondered why in a country with an English newspaper tradition that goes back more than 100 years, I have to depend on journalism textbooks by British and American writers. Their books explain efficiently how to compose a good lead, edit correctly and write an expressive headline. But their context is invariably western and far too often what these writers have to say sounds strange and inappropriate to the Indian ear.

I am glad that Sunil Saxena—who has a long and envious career in journalism with some of India's most honoured newspapers and magazines—has filled this gap with a most useful book on headline writing.

The earliest newspapers had no headlines on the front page, which was devoted entirely to advertisements, and the headlines inside did no more than announce the subject of the report. Hence, the headline of an Iraq War report, written in traditional style—on the fall of Baghdad to coalition forces—would probably be 'Fall of Baghdad', followed by 'Coalition Forces Success' and 'Saddam Still at Large'.

What Saxena's book will teach you is that if luring the reader is the goal of headline writers, they would succeed if their headline read 'Baghdad Falls', followed by 'Coalition Forces Enter City' and 'Saddam Hussein Escapes Enemy Dragnet'.

That is what Saxena does best—imparting the knowledge he has acquired during an impressive career to the neophyte who wants to be initiated into the mystery of writing arresting headlines.

It comes almost as a letdown when the reader learns at the end of Saxena's well-produced and easy-to-read book that there is no mystery to writing headlines. Granted it is one of the most difficult tasks that sub-editors face, but by following Saxena's guidelines and explanations, coupled with a determination never to settle for anything but the best, sub-editors should be able to achieve a level of competency that would make them a welcome addition to any newspaper desk.

Saxena explains in a very readable fashion the jargon of headlinese—the language of Headlines—in the Glossary. The list of terms used casually and frequently by sub-editors poring over columns of copy at the editing desk includes words that derive from British and American newspapers which is most useful in India where sub-editors use a mixture of these terms.

A most useful element in Saxena's book is the clarity with which he breaks headlines down to their basic elements and explains how these should be assembled to produce effective headlines. One of his chapters describes different kinds of headlines and the means – kickers, straplines, crossheads, among others – that sub-editors employ to support their headlines.

Another chapter explains the art of writing headlines for feature articles. Stressing that feature headlines are the most creative form of headline writing, Saxena makes it a point to emphasize that it is creativity that requires the maximum effort from the sub-editor.

Saxena even provides a list of do's and don'ts in headline writing that neophytes would do well to absorb and follow. They are not offered as rules – for there is nothing engraved in stone on writing headlines – but more as tips, accumulated during a long and varied career. That his experience in journalism includes two stints as a teacher of the craft surely helped Saxena to keep in mind that though he was writing a book, he was in fact a teacher detailing to a class of eager students the requirements of writing headlines, the frustration that results when synonyms and antonyms are hard to come by and the overwhelming pleasure that is triggered by a headline that the writer knows qualifies by any standard as an excellent one.

Saxena has not neglected the task of the journalist working as in the electronic media. One of the chapters is devoted to the craft of writing headlines for online reports. This chapter is especially instructive because it draws on the years that Saxena has been guiding the online version of the *New Indian Express*, one of India's major national newspapers.

PROF. K.T. OOMMEN
Director
Manorama School of Communication
Kottayam

Preface

Headlines test the skills of the best desk professionals. There are a few blessed souls to whom headlines occur in a flash; but there are countless others who struggle to write one. I do not blame them. Headlines have a nasty habit of not coming to mind when they are needed most. There are also times when the hard pressed copy editor finds a good headline, but it is either too long or too short to fit the assigned space.

Headlines can be a nightmare for the most experienced desk professionals. For the beginners they are Chinese torture. One reason why headline writers tie themselves in knots is because they learn the craft of headline writing by trial and error; there are no Indian texts that teach it. The best that the editing books do is to devote one or two chapters to the cause of headline writing.

Like all beginners I too gnawed my nails and wracked my mind — often without success — to write 'good' headlines. With time, I learnt some of the short cuts that the seniors used. These short cuts, called headlinese, are standard verbs that are used time and again because they take less space and can fit a variety of situations.

But this was only a limited solution. A couple of teaching stints gave me a chance to look at headlines with a little less rancour. It was then that I realized that headlines need not be treated like cryptic clues. They can be written far more easily if one understood a simple fact — all that a headline needs is a noun and an active verb.

This was a great discovery for a person who had suffered the ignominy of seeing several of his 'best' headlines rejected. I then dug deeper and saw the wisdom of some of the 'headline tricks' that have been passed by one generation of headline writers to another. I also found some other 'bright nuggets' that could be put together to demystify the task of headline writing.

The result of these efforts is this book. The book treats headline writing as a craft that can be learnt from a teacher in a classroom or from an individual's own efforts on a newspaper desk. The book also provides extensive exercises for teachers to help students of journalism master the craft of headline writing.

This is the aim of the book. How far I have succeeded in my venture is something only you can judge.

Good Luck.

SUNIL SAXENA

Acknowledgements

This book would not have been possible without the support that was extended by Mr Manoj Kumar Sonthalia, Chairman-cum-Managing Director of The New Indian Express Group. The *New Indian Express* is probably the only media house in India that encourages its staff members to undertake such ventures.

I am also thankful to Mr Sonthalia for allowing the use of news reports published in the *New Indian Express*. These reports have been used in the section on headline writing exercises, and are credited with the legendary Express News Service or ENS byline.

I would also like to thank the General Manager of United News of India (UNI), Mr M.K. Laul, for allowing the use of UNI reports in the section on headline writing exercises. All these reports are credited to UNI.

The Press Trust of India (PTI) was equally magnanimous. Mr Vijay S. Satokar, Deputy Editor, Special Services, was very prompt in extending permission to use reports generated by his agency. These reports have been used under the PTI byline.

I would also like to thank the Editor-in-Charge of the *Week*, Mr T.R. Gopalakrishnan. He showed no hesitation in granting permission for the use of interviews published in the *Week*. The interviews have been credited to the *Week*.

The book also uses several reports/features produced by Indo-Asian News Service (IANS). For this I am deeply thankful to Mr K.P.K. Kutty, who has always encouraged me in my work. All these reports have been credited to IANS.

Last but not the least, I would like to thank Prof. K.T. Oommen, Director, Manorama School of Communication, for writing the Foreword. Prof. Oommen is one of the finest journalism educators in the country and his words hold great value for me.

The book also carries scores of examples that have been sourced from different Indian newspapers. These examples have been used to explain the headline writing techniques in an impartial and unbiased manner. They are no reflection on the quality of any newspaper but random samples to illustrate technical points.

Abbreviations

BJP	Bharatiya Janata Party
BSP	Bahujan Samaj Party
CBI	Central Bureau of Investigation
CPI(M)	Communist Party of India (Marxist)
DGP	Director General of Police
EBC	Economically Backward Class
ENS	Express News Service
FDI	Foreign Direct Investment
IHF	Indian Hockey Federation
NASSCOM	National Association of Software and Service Companies
NCERT	National Council of Educational Research and Training
NDA	National Democratic Alliance
NDTV	New Delhi Television Limited
NGO	Non-governmental organization
POTA	Prevention of Terrorism Act
PTI	Press Trust of India
UNI	United News of India
UPA	United Progressive Alliance
VAT	Value Added Tax

1

Headline and its Functions

A headline, in its most elementary form, can be described as the title of a news report set in big and bold letters. But this is too elementary a definition. A good headline is one that in less than a dozen words summarizes what a reporter has said in 100, 250 or even 500 words. These few words, when set on top of a news report in display type, that is big letters, work as the reader's guide, compass and index. They spark curiosity and draw readers into a story, establish news value and relative importance of a news report, provide contrast and balance on a page and give character and identity to a publication.

Good copy editors spend considerable time in writing headlines. They realize that dead and dull headlines drive readers away from good news reports. They also realize that the best headlines are crafted by hard work through skills learnt in journalism schools and newspaper desks—against deadline pressures. New technology and the modernization of the newspaper have only added to the pressure. A headline writer is now expected to write more creative, imaginative, even commentative headlines. He is also expected to think colour when visualizing a headline.

While these pressures were there in the past, they were limited. The biggest constraint was the availability of display types, that is, the types used to write headlines. A newspaper had to work with a small selection of typefaces, often with only one. There was no variation possible as these types were cast in metal and mounted on wooden blocks. There were occasions when a newspaper, in the absence of good quality types, was forced to use worn out typefaces as their availability was limited.

Headlines in Pre-independence Days

Indian newspapers, during the first half of the twentieth century, used headlines written in small points over reports set in narrow columns. Headlines set in large display type were limited largely to the top half of the page. A good example is the front page of the *Hindustan Times* dated 9 October 1924 (Fig. 1.1). The page started off with a banner headline set in all capitals that announced that Mahatma

Fig. 1.1: *The front page of the* Hindustan Times *dated 9 October 1924. The page looked like a grey sheet of text as multicolumn headlines were limited to the top half of the page.*

Gandhi had broken his fast. There were two other display headlines, once again near the top of the page. The rest of the page was a mass of grey. A similar display can be seen in the *Hindu* dated 15 August 1947 (Fig. 1.2).

Another interesting point noticed in the Indian newspapers of this time was the use of decks. The headline was not a single element but was made of several decks, each deck separated from another by a thin rule. This is how the *Hindu's* main headline read on 15 August 1947:

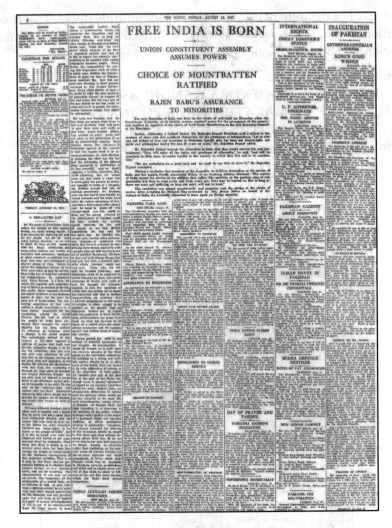

Fig. 1.2: *The front page of the* Hindu *announcing the birth of free India. The newspaper used headlines across the page to break the greyness of the text. The headlines were in small points and the intention clearly was to accommodate as much information as possible.*

Main headline:	**FREE INDIA IS BORN**
First deck:	**UNION CONSTITUENT ASSEMBLY ASSUMES POWER**
Second deck:	**CHOICE OF MOUNTBATTEN RATIFIED**
Third deck:	**RAJEN BABU'S ASSURANCE TO MINORITIES**

the *Hindu* was not the only newspaper that used multiple decks. The *Times of India* in its edition dated 31 January 1948 (Fig. 1.3) used four decks to announce the assassination of Mahatma Gandhi:

Banner headline and
the main deck: **MAHATMA GANDHI ASSASSINATED AT DELHI**
First deck: **MARATHA FROM POONA FIRES**
                        AT POINT-BLANK RANGE
Second deck: **Outrage On Way To Prayer Meeting**
Third deck: **FUNERAL TODAY AT JUMNA GHAT:**
                        COUNTRY-WIDE GRIEF

Fig. 1.3: *The* Times of India's *front page announcing Mahatma Gandhi's assassination. Headlines set in multiple decks are one of the dominant features of the page.*

However, unlike the *Hindu*, the *Times of India* used decks set in all capitals and in upper-lower case to provide contrast.

The use of decks was not limited to the lead or the most important story of the day. The *Times of India* used them in multicolumn headlines displayed in the lower half of the page (Fig. 1.4) also. The *Mail* (Fig. 1.5) too used decks both in single column and multicolumn settings.

Fig. 1.4: *The* Times of India's *front page announcing India's independence. This was a busy front page as it used both photographs and multicolumn headlines. A highlight of the page was the use of decks in both single column and multicolumn headlines.*

22

Fig. 1.5: *The* Mail, *which stopped publication in the last quarter of the twentieth century, used deck headlines to provide contrast on the page.*

Post-independence Headlines
(1951–80)

The decks started falling into disuse after independence. The first to go were decks used with single column headlines. Later, editors started dropping them from multicolumn headlines and limited their use to major events or news breaks such as wars, earthquakes, assassinations, budget presentations or election results. Even here, decks were confined to headlines that ran on top of the page, especially as props for banner headlines.

We must remember that this was a period of status quo. The journalism was staid and there were virtually no innovations. The hot metal printing system did not allow editors to experiment with headline styles. There was also a shortage of display type and newspapers preferred to use only one font family.

Desktop Publishing Era (1980s Onwards)

The arrival of desktop publishing and the evolution of modular makeup had a dramatic impact on the way headlines were written and displayed. The stress was to eliminate clutter on news pages; the first casualty was multiple decks. These were replaced by single line shoulders or kickers written in small points on top of the main headline (see Chapter 5).

Another development was the emergence of the strapline as an important constituent of the headline. This change was introduced by the *Indian Express* in the second half of the 1990s, and was later adopted by other major newspapers like the *Times of India* and the *Hindustan Times*. The strapline was written to highlight important points that could not be covered in the main headline.

Yet another interesting development was the use of colour in headlines. Magazines were the first to do so and later newspapers too started setting headlines in colour. The *Hindustan Times* went a step further and introduced a new trend by using colour to highlight select words within a headline.

These were not the only innovations that resulted from new technology. Another development was the setting of headlines in reverse; this allowed editors to use white letters against a black background (Fig. 1.6). As technology advanced, newspapers started using colour screens to display headlines; we can expect these innovations to continue as technology adds more tools to the newspaper editor's toolbox.

Some of the earlier headline styles could also return as newspapers compete for attention. The *Asian Age*, in its edition dated 19 October 2004, used decks to announce the killing of Veerappan, a notorious sandalwood smuggler, a style that had virtually fallen into disuse for quite sometime (Fig. 1.7).

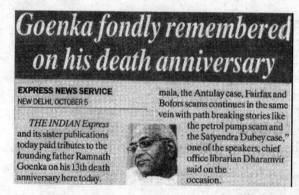

Fig. 1.6: *A headline in reverse setting used by the* Indian Express. *The letters are in white on a black background.*

Fig. 1.7: *A headline using multiple decks as a shoulder in the* Asian Age.

FUNCTIONS OF A HEADLINE

The tools may change and the editors may become more adventurous but one thing that will remain constant is the role of a headline. Headlines have traditionally performed six major functions and they will continue to do so in the future. These six functions are discussed below.

Index the News

The three news elements that arrest eye movement on a newspaper page are photographs, graphics and headlines. Of these, photographs and graphics tell a story visually while headlines tell a story in words. The number of words used to relate the story may be few but when taken together they work as a valuable index. They guide readers to stories of their interest, add to their reading pleasure and help them save time as they flip through different pages. That is why headlines are compared to beacons; they chart a reader's course across large masses of grey text.

Establish News Value

Headlines help readers judge the relative importance of a news report. This is not easily achieved because the reader has no formal training in gauging the true import of stories merely by looking at headlines. Much depends on the consistency of the headline writers in developing this awareness.

There are four navigational tools used to develop such consciousness among readers. These are:

Headline Width

The first is the width of the headline, that is, the number of columns used to write a headline. This depends on three factors.

Story length

The length of a story is directly proportional to its news value. A news report in one or two paragraphs obviously does not have much value in the newspaper's opinion. Such a story will be displayed in a single column only, as happened in the case of two Chinese engineers who were kidnapped in Pakistan (Fig. 1.8). The report did not have much news value for Indian readers and was allotted two paragraphs. The headline was set in a small point size to reinforce the message. In contrast, stories that are displayed across two or more columns obviously are more important (Fig. 1.9).

Story positioning

The most important news reports are positioned at the top of the page (Fig. 1.10). The less important ones are placed in the middle or the bottom half of the page.

2 Chinese engineers kidnapped in Pak

Islambad, Oct 9: Suspected Islamic militants today kidnapped two Chinese engineers and their two Pakistani guards in Pakistan's troubled South Waziristan tribal area bordering Afghanistan, where security forces were involved in operations to flush out al Qaeda militants.

Fig. 1.8: *The report of two Chinese engineers kidnapped in Pakistan did not have much news value for Indian readers. A single column headline set in a small point size was used to report the event.*

Fig. 1.9: *The newspaper assigned eight inches of space spread across four columns for this news report. Clearly, the newspaper considered the news report to be important for its readers.*

Service tax target fixed at Rs 1,650 cr

Express News Service

Chennai, Oct 9: The Commissionerate of Service Tax, Chennai, is targeting an increase of nearly Rs 1,000 crore in revenue mobilisation during the current financial year. Chief Commissioner of Central Excise J Sridharan said today. Addressing the media, Sridharan said from Rs 680 crore during the last financial year, the Commissionerate was looking at generating Rs 1,650 crore during the current year. The current collection figures (up to September) stands at Rs 408 crore, he said.

Pointing out that the strategy towards achieving this target was a twin tier one, Sridharan said, "As the first step the Chennai Commissionerate, which includes Chennai, Chennai Zone III and Pondicherry, would work towards the disposal of all adjudication cases pending wherein only the technicalities are involved with the waiver of penalty. "The second measure aims to bring those service providers who unknowingly or unintentionally could not register themselves as service tax assessees in the earlier years by providing an opportunity to register now without any questions being asked about their past liability and without penalising them for the delay," he explained.

According to him, with the addition of 12 new services to the list of services liable for tax with effect from Sunday, the Commissionerate would organise camps at various locations in the city to enable service providers falling under these newly-mentioned categories to get themselves registered. "These camps would also provide an opportunity for on the spot adjudication of cases of technical nature involving only penalty up to November 30, 2004," he said.

The addition of 12 new services which include business exhibition services, airport services, transport of goods by air, survey and exploration of minerals, opinion poll services, intellectual property services, forward contract services and outdoor or canteen services, among others, now takes the total of taxable services to 71. The camps would be held at the following locations: On October 11 and 28 the venues would be Nungambakkam and Nandanam, on October 14 at Parrys, T Nagar, Anna Nagar and Adyar, on October 18 at Tiruvottiyur, Egmore, Mylapore and Porur, on October 20 at Parrys, Anna Nagar, Egmore, Nanganallur, on October 26 at Tiruvottiyur, Mylapore, T Nagar and Velachery.

Officials at the Commissionerate also added that any service provider was free to approach any of the camps irrespective of the jurisdiction for appropriate guidance. For further information contact - Ph: 24331177, 24330066 (Extn: 671), 24330666 (extn:111) or kalaichennai@tn.nic.in

The only exception to this rule is the anchor, a soft story placed at the base of the front page. The reader may not be aware of the anchor's value, but it is one report that is assigned the highest priority in most newspapers (Fig. 1.11). It plays two major roles: one, it helps to bind the base of the page with a multicolumn item; and two, it provides variety since it is the only soft story on the front page—the rest are all hard news reports.

Relative importance of a story

This is not an easy yardstick. Even the most seasoned newsmen flounder when judging the relative importance of news stories. This is because a news report may qualify for a multicolumn display based on its importance and length, but it may still be run as a deep single column because the other stories are far more important and need better display. Only very discerning readers are able to comprehend this point (see also Chapter 2).

Fig. 1.10: *The top half of a news page where the most important stories of the day have been placed. All the headlines have been set in big point sizes.*

Fig. 1.11: *A soft report run as an anchor at the base of the front page.*

Point Size

The point size is as important in establishing the importance of a news report as the width of a headline. The reader may not know it but the term 'point' dates back to the hot metal printing era. The largest point size in use then was 72 and the smallest point size was one. To make it easier for typographers, one point was defined as a dot equivalent to 1/72 of an inch. On this scale, 72 points was the highest point size and was equal to an inch. Today computers have made it possible to set types in much larger point sizes.

Considerable thought goes into the selection of point size. The most important deciding factor is the headline width. The point size will be small if the news report is to be run across a single column. A big point size will be jarring to the eye, especially if it is bigger than the point size used for multicolumn headlines. Newspaper design demands a certain proportion in the way point sizes are chosen to display news reports. There will be a mismatch if a single column headline is written in 28 points and a three-column headline is in 14 points as shown in Fig. 1.12.

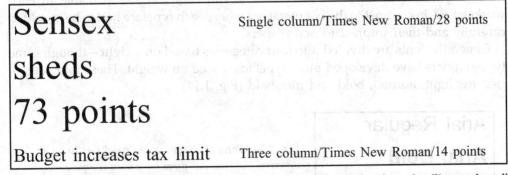

Fig. 1.12: *There will be a mismatch if a large point size is used for single column headlines and small point size for multicolumn headlines.*

The second most important deciding factor is the importance of a story. The news desk may decide to run two news reports as single column items but it will underscore their news value by using headlines set in different point sizes. For instance, a Delhi newspaper used a headline set in 20 points to report the killing of four soldiers in a fidayeen attack in Kashmir, but chose 14 points for the headline announcing the arrest of a killer (Fig. 1.13).

Four killed in attack on army camp

Single column/Times New Roman/20 points

LU Professor's killer arrested

Single column/Times New Roman/14 points

Fig. 1.13: *Two headlines written in different point sizes for single column news reports. Clearly, the newspaper attached more importance to the first story.*

Readers use the same yardstick in making their value judgements. They realize that the point size of a story is directly proportional to its importance.

Headline Weight

Before bringing out the importance of weight in headline writing it is important to understand what 'weight' is. The weight of a typeface is decided by how 'black' the typeface is. The one that is blacker is said to be heavier. Desktop publishing has made it possible to have the same font in different weights available in each workstation, in contrast to the hot metal era where each typeface had to be moulded carefully and then shipped to newspapers.

Generally, fonts are divided into four categories based on weight—though some typographers have developed more typefaces based on weight. These four categories are: light, normal, bold and ultrabold (Fig. 1.14).

Arial Regular

Arial Bold

Arial Ultrabold

Fig. 1.14: *Three headlines of the Arial family set in different weights. All three have been composed in 16 points, but Arial Ultrabold stands out on account of its heaviness or blackness.*

However, to avoid clutter on a newspaper page designers insist that the 'weight' choices be limited. That is why Indian newspapers commonly prefer to use regular and bold formats only. The regular weight is used for most headlines while the bold format is used for headlines that need special display; the latter catches a reader's eye more quickly than the former.

Once again readers are able to judge the news value of a story without knowing the thinking that goes into selecting the headline weight. They realize that a bolder weight means a more important story. Let us look at two reports that were filed on the ICC Cup 2004. The first was a soft report and gave details about the ticket rush for the India-Pakistan match; the second was a hard news report and gave the grim news that Sachin Tendulkar would not be playing in the prestigious tournament. The second report had more news value and this was reflected in the bolder typeface selected for the headline (Fig. 1.15).

Big rush for Indo-Pak match	Single Column, Times New Roman, Regular, 14 points
Tendulkar to miss ICC Cup	Single Column, Times New Roman, Bold, 14 points

Fig. 1.15: *Clearly, the second story had a much higher news value than the first.*

Headline Style

This is another small flourish that allows readers to judge the news value of a report. The two most commonly used headline styles are regular and italics. The regular typeface, which is popularly known as the roman typeface, is made of straight letters. In contrast, italics is a typeface that is made of slanted or sloping letters.

The headline writer uses italics to draw attention to a light or amusing story (Fig. 1.16). Another advantage of italics is that it provides contrast on the page. However, it should be used selectively; excessive use will confuse the reader and the advantage of using contrasting letters will be lost.

ESPN takes cablemen on a costly ride	Regular
Poodles have a busy day	*Italics*

Fig. 1.16: *The headline writer conveys the light mood of the poodles' story by choosing italics as the typeface.*

These four navigation tools — width, size, weight and style — when used with care and consistency become the foremost guide of readers in judging the news value of a story. They may not understand their mechanics but they are able to understand the message that headlines convey.

Depict the Mood of the Story

Headlines reflect emotions such as anger, joy or sadness by using appropriate adjectives or adverbs. In 2003, Prime Minister Atal Behari Vajpayee gave a hard-hitting speech in the United Nations rebutting the statements made by President Pervez Musharraf of Pakistan. The *Times of India* captured Vajpayee's anger brilliantly in its headline (Fig. 1.17). One look at the headline and the reader would have understood the thrust of Vajpayee's speech.

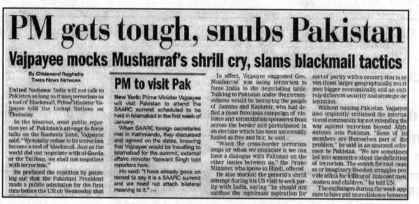

Fig. 1.17: *The verbs 'tough', 'mocks' and 'slam' capture the mood of the story.*

Another headline that reflected the story writer's exasperation was the one related to the ICC Champions Cup 2004 whose format allowed USA and Bangladesh to compete against the world's top cricket playing nations. The matches were so one-sided and predictable that the tournament lost its sheen and excitement. The headline writer captured this sentiment by using the word 'jokers' for the relatively new cricket playing nations (Fig. 1.18).

Fig. 1.18: *The comment is harsh, but it reflects the mood of the writer's opinion of the first leg of the ICC Champions Trophy 2004.*

Set the Tone of the Newspaper

Headlines are the first indicator of a newspaper's policy. A tabloid generally prefers to use bold headlines set in big point size (Fig. 1.19), whereas a mainstream newspaper that wants to convey a conservative image uses smaller point sizes and a quieter tone (Fig. 1.20).

Fig. 1.19: *The headline used by a Delhi-based tabloid to announce the arrest of a tantrik who had political connections.*

> # Arrested
>
> **Godman's evil days are over;
> Court takes it upon itself
> to clip tantrik's wings**

In contrast, a mainstream newspaper's headline had a more sedate tone.

> # Tantrik arrested in Delhi, sent to judicial custody

Fig. 1.20: *The tone and display of the tantrik's arrest in a Delhi mainstream newspaper was quieter and conservative.*

Several large-selling tabloids like *Mid-Day* use headlines set in large points on their cover page (Fig. 1.21) and smaller or normal point sizes on inside pages. The large point size helps the newspaper to catch the eyes of commuters in Mumbai and Delhi.

Provide Typographical Relief

Headlines constitute an important visual tool in brightening the newspaper. They provide typographical relief and make the page look livelier and more attractive, sometimes even without photographs (Fig. 1.22). That is why editors, and now designers, take so much pain in identifying the typeface for headlines. The stress is on choosing a font that adds both weight and character to a newspaper and makes it visually more appealing.

Headlines are also used to provide contrast on the page. A bold headline will be set against a light headline to add to the visual appeal of a page (Fig. 1.23 and Fig. 1.24.)

Give Identity

Headlines lend a distinct character and identity to a newspaper. Readers get accustomed to the typeface and the size of headlines used in their daily newspapers.

32

Fig. 1.21: *A front page of* Mid-Day.

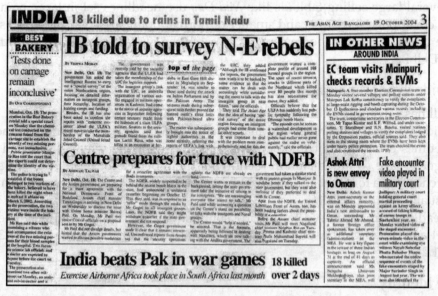

Fig. 1.22: *Headlines provide typographical relief on the page. The newspaper has used no photograph but has relied upon headlines set in large point sizes to provide contrast.*

Advani ascension: Mixed response from RSS, VHP

Indo-EU summit on November 8

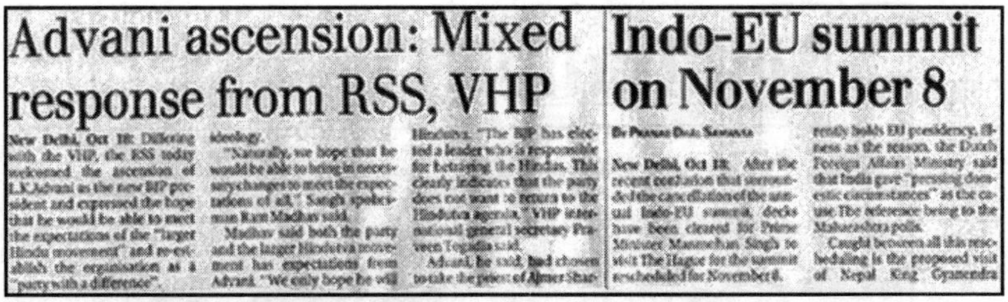

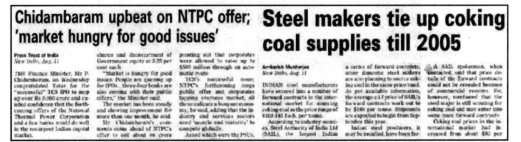

Fig. 1.23: *A bold headline is placed next to a light headline to provide contrast on an inside page of a newspaper.*

Chidambaram upbeat on NTPC offer; 'market hungry for good issues'

Steel makers tie up coking coal supplies till 2005

Fig. 1.24: *The* Business Line, *which runs multicolumn news reports side by side, varies the typeface to ensure that the headlines are not read as one. Also, the typestyle adopted provides contrast on the page.*

That is why newspapers do not experiment with headlines; the paper's identity may be lost in the reader's mind. They use standard typefaces and point sizes in writing headlines and insist that these are followed.

The *New Indian Express* changed its headline and body font on 1 September 2004 to make the paper look livelier and more vibrant. The design change was entrusted to a well-known designer and was carried out after much deliberation by the newspaper's top editors and managers. The result was very pleasing to the eye. But there must have been readers who felt a little flustered the day they got their first copy of the redesigned paper. The change was very evident and can be easily noticed from the front page of the Chennai edition of the *New Indian Express* before it changed the body and headline font (Fig. 1.25) and after (Fig. 1.26).

Popular Headline Terms

Newspapers have spawned their own headline lingo. Some of these terms are used commonly across newspapers; but some like 'shoulder' or 'strapline' can have different meanings in different newspapers. But broadly, the following are used to indicate different terms associated with headlines:

Fig. 1.25: *The front page before the body and headline fonts were changed.*

Banner/Streamer

This is a headline that is run across all eight columns on top of the front page. The banner is used for momentous events and is set in big and bold letters. It is also referred to as a streamer. When Veerappan, a notorious sandalwood smuggler and forest brigand with over 150 killings against his name, was shot dead by the Special Task Force, the *New Indian Express* used a banner to announce his death (Fig. 1.27).

35

Headline and its Functions

Fig. 1.26: *The front page after the body and headline fonts were changed.*

Fig. 1.27: *A banner headline used to announce the killing of Veerappan in the* New Indian Express.

Downstyle

It is the system of capitalization where the first letter of a headline, the first letter of proper nouns and acronyms are set in capital letters (Fig. 1.28). This is the most popular form of headline writing practised in India.

In contrast, some newspapers today have started using the first letter of every word in capitals. No specific term is used for this style of headline writing. But this is not considered a healthy practice since capital letters use more space (strapline used in Fig. 1.28).

Headlines can also be set in an all-capital format. This headline style is particularly favoured by the *Asian Age* (Fig. 1.29).

Fig. 1.28: *The main headline has been written using the downstyle system of capitalization. The first letter of the headline and the acronym PM are in capitals; the rest of the letters are in lower case. In contrast, in the strapline the first letter of every word is in capitals.*

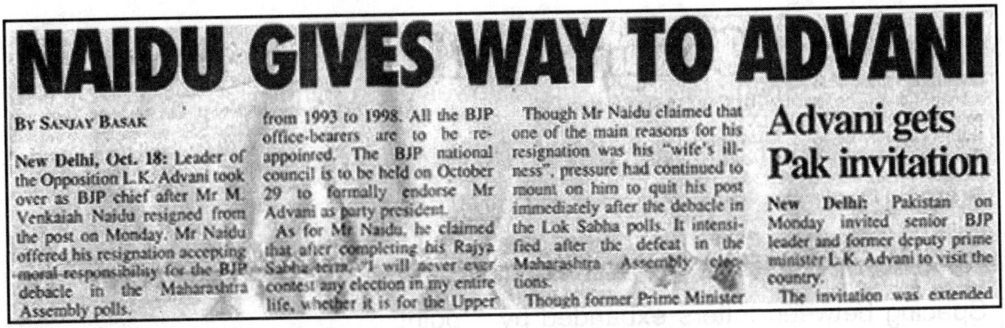

NAIDU GIVES WAY TO ADVANI

By Sanjay Basak

New Delhi, Oct. 18: Leader of the Opposition L.K. Advani took over as BJP chief after Mr M. Venkaiah Naidu resigned from the post on Monday. Mr Naidu offered his resignation accepting moral responsibility for the BJP debacle in the Maharashtra Assembly polls.

from 1993 to 1998. All the BJP office-bearers are to be re-appointed. The BJP national council is to be held on October 29 to formally endorse Mr Advani as party president.

As for Mr Naidu, he claimed that after completing his Rajya Sabha term, "I will never ever contest any election in my entire life, whether it is for the Upper

Though Mr Naidu claimed that one of the main reasons for his resignation was his "wife's illness", pressure had continued to mount on him to quit his post immediately after the debacle in the Lok Sabha polls. It intensified after the defeat in the Maharashtra Assembly elections.

Though former Prime Minister

Advani gets Pak invitation

New Delhi: Pakistan on Monday invited senior BJP leader and former deputy prime minister L.K. Advani to visit the country.

The invitation was extended

Fig. 1.29: *A headline set in all-capitals in the* Asian Age.

Font

Font is a full set of characters/letters available in a specific weight/style in a family. It includes all letters of alphabets, numerals and punctuation marks both in capitals and upper/lower case.

Headline Width

This means the number of columns across which a headline runs.

Headline Weight

The weight of a typeface depends on its blackness. The one that is blacker is said to have a heavier weight (Fig. 1.14).

Italics

These are gently sloping letters with or without serifs. They may have thick and thin stems or uniform stems, but their distinguishing characteristic remains their slanted letters (Fig. 1.16). Newspapers set headlines in italics to display a light or a non-serious story. The credit of developing the italics typeface goes to Aldus Manutius.

Kern

It is a term used to denote the condensation or expansion of space between characters that make a word. It is also defined as the horizontal scaling of text. Kerning is a useful tool when used sparingly. Excessive kerning can distort a font and reduce its value or utility (Fig. 1.30). That is why it is considered most suitable for feature headlines or for headlines for magazine articles, where a font can be kerned to reflect the mood of a story.

15 pilgrims from Tamil Nadu die as bus falls into gorge
Times New Roman, 14 points, upper-lower no kerning.

15 pilgrims from Tamil Nadu die as bus falls into gorge
Spacing between letters condensed by 1 point.

15 pilgrims from Tamil Nadu die as bus falls into gorge
Spacing between letters expanded by 1 point.

15 pilgrims from Tamil Nadu die as bus falls into gorge
Horizontal scaling 200%.

15 pilgrims from Tamil Nadu die as bus falls into gorge
Horizontal scaling 50%.

Fig. 1.30: *Headlines can be kerned to squeeze or expand words. An example of how a headline written in Times New Roman, 14 points, upper-lower is altered using different kerning techniques.*

Kicker/Shoulder

This is the headline that is written on top of the main headline (Fig. 1.31). It is set in a point size that is less than one used to write the main headline. It was initially used to indicate the subject of a news story but now it is used to highlight news points not covered in the main headline. In several newspapers the kicker is also called a shoulder.

NUTRITION IN SCHOOLS / HOMEMADE FOOD LOSING OUT

It's media that decides what your child eats

By Our Staff Reporter

CHENNAI, OCT. 13. Children are 'picky' eaters and difficult to please. But there are ways to get around that if parents and teachers apply their mind.

week as schoolteachers, nutritionists and consumer activists debated the nutrition status of children in private and State-funded schools.

Taste, image and a preference for brand names take prec-

quality of drinking water in seven schools was suspect because of the water shortage in the city. Though school curricula stressed natural, healthy food, insufficient funds and indifferent menus led to children refus-

Fig. 1.31: *A shoulder or kicker used by the* Hindu *to provide more information in the headline.*

Point

It is a measurement unit used to indicate type sizes. The point system was designed by Pierre Fournier in 1837 and which is in use, with slight modifications, even today. One point is equal to 1/72 of an inch or 0.0138 inches.

Point Size

It is the height of a typeface.

Reverse

In this typesetting style, the letters are white and the background is grey or black (Fig. 1.26). Today, it is possible to compose letters in a wide variety of colours; similarly, the background colours can be changed to make the type stand out.

Reverse Shoulder/Strapline

This is the headline written beneath the main headline in a smaller point size than that used to write the main headline. It is generally used to highlight a new point and can also be used to amplify the main headline. In some newspapers, reverse shoulder is also referred to as a strapline (Fig. 1.32).

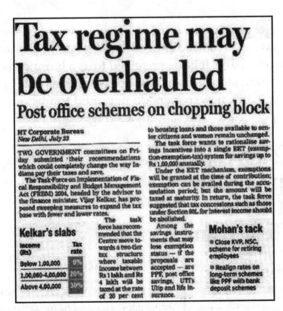

Fig. 1.32: *A strapline or reverse shoulder used below the main headline in the* Hindustan Times.

Roman Letters

These are upright letters with thick and thin stems with small, line strokes known as serifs. The credit of developing Roman letters goes to a Frenchman, Nicholas Jenson, who developed them while working in Italy in the fifteenth century.

Standing Heads

These are headlines that are not changed every day. They are used for regular items like weather, city diary, etc., and are also known as stet heads (Fig. 1.33).

Fig. 1.33: *A standing or stet head 'From the Diary…' used in the* Hindu.

Sub-head

It is a one or two-word headline that is inserted at the head of a paragraph to break the monotony of a solid column of type. It is also written as a headline for items that are strung together like city briefs. Sub-heads are generally written in bold letters in the same point size as the body text.

Tombstone

A tombstone results when two headlines of the same point size and the same width are run side by side on a page. It is also referred to as a bumped headline (Fig. 1.34). Most editors avoid tombstones on newspaper pages as the headlines read into each other. However, some newspapers do not mind tombstones; they lessen their impact by using typefaces of different styles (Fig. 1.35).

Fig. 1.34: *Two single column headlines written in the same point size and in the same number of decks placed next to each other in the* Asian Age. *This is a classic example of tombstoning and should be avoided.*

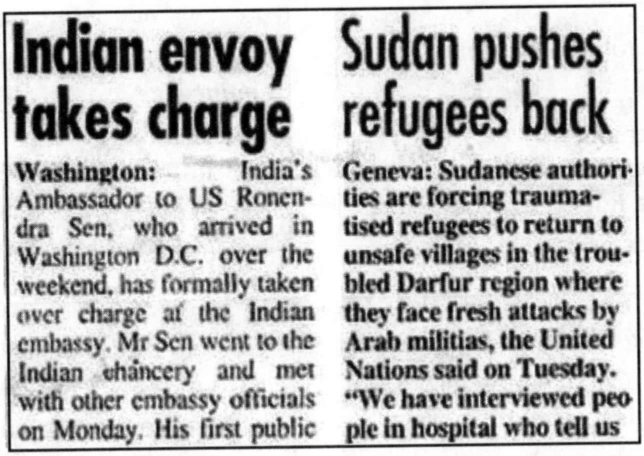

Indian envoy takes charge

Washington: India's Ambassador to US Ronendra Sen, who arrived in Washington D.C. over the weekend, has formally taken over charge at the Indian embassy. Mr Sen went to the Indian chancery and met with other embassy officials on Monday. His first public

Sudan pushes refugees back

Geneva: Sudanese authorities are forcing traumatised refugees to return to unsafe villages in the troubled Darfur region where they face fresh attacks by Arab militias, the United Nations said on Tuesday. "We have interviewed people in hospital who tell us

Fig. 1.35: *A bold and a light typeface used to provide contrast on the page and separate two headlines that are run side by side in the* Asian Age.

Sans Serifs

Sans serifs are typefaces whose individual strokes are of the same width. They do not end in a tiny, decorative stroke. Their stark character makes them suitable for writing headlines.

Serifs

These typefaces use decorative flourishes at the end of main strokes to lend elegance to the character. They are used for body settings as they give the vision of continuity.

Chapter Highlights

The six functions of a headline

1. Index the news.
2. Establish news value.
3. Depict the mood of the story.
4. Set the tone of the newspaper.
5. Provide typographical relief.
6. Give identity.

Tools used to establish news value

1. Headline width.
2. Point size.
3. Headline weight.
4. Headline style.

Tools used to decide column width

1. Story length.
2. Story positioning.
3. Relative importance of a story.

Parameters used to decide point size

1. Headline width.
2. Importance of a story.
3. Relative importance of a story.

How to select headline weight

1. Use regular typeface, also known as roman, for normal stories.
2. Use heavy or bold typeface for very important stories.
3. Use light typeface for soft stories.
4. Do not use a smattering of weights on a single page.

How to decide headline style

1. Use roman or straight letters are used for regular news reports.
2. Use sloping letters or italics for light stories.

How headlines establish the identity of a newspaper

1. Mainstream newspapers use conservative point sizes to write headlines.
2. Tabloids use large, screaming headlines.
3. Combative newspapers use strong verbs to comment on issues.

Depicting the mood of the story

1. Use appropriate verbs, adjectives or adverbs.
2. Use italics for light stories.
3. Use bold typeface for important stories.

Headlines as a design tool

1. Provide typographical relief by breaking large chunks of text.
2. Provide contrast by using bold and light faces.

HEADLINE EXERCISES

Exercise 1

Please go through the day's newspaper and select five news reports based on the following guidelines:
  i)   One single column headline with a single deck.*
  ii) One single column headline with two decks.
  iii) One single column headline with three or four decks.
  iv) One single column headline written in italics.
  v)   One single column headline written in bold.

Examine each headline closely to find out what functions the headline may have served on the newspaper page. Then use the format given below to list its characteristics:
  i)   Write the headline in full.
  ii)   Format: single column, two decks/single column, three decks/single column, four decks.
  iii) Positioning: top half of the page/bottom half of the page/top of the column.
  iv)   Point size: small/large.
  v)   Story length: one/two/three/four/five paragraphs or more.
  vi)   Weight: light/bold/roman.
  vii) Style: straight letters/italics.
  viii) Mood: serious/light.
  ix)   Tone: conservative/angry/flippant.

Exercise 2

Please go through last week's newspapers and locate headlines that depict the mood of the story either:
  i) Through words that reflect emotions, or
  ii) Through font style.

Exercise 3

Please go through last week's broadsheet and tabloid newspapers and locate headlines that reflect the publication's tone. You may use the following yardsticks to establish the tone of a publication:
  i)   Point size.
  ii) Choice of words.
  iii) Headline display.

* The deck in this context means the number of lines. Thus, a single column headline with three decks means a headline that has three lines.

Exercise 4

Please go through one week's newspapers and locate headlines that are used to provide contrast on the page.

Exercise 5

Please go through last week's newspapers and select eight news reports based on the following guidelines:

  i) Two reports whose headlines are written across one column.
  ii) Two reports whose headlines are written across two columns.
  iii) One report whose headline straddles three columns but has a single deck.
  iv) One report whose headline straddles three columns but has two decks.
  v) One report whose headline is written in italics.
  vi) One report that has been used as a lead story.

Use the given format to list what function(s) each headline served. Also, give your reasons for reaching the conclusion using the guidelines listed for each function.

  i) Establish news value.
     Width.
     Story length
     Story positioning
     Relative importance of a story

     Point size.
     Small
     Large

     Weight.
     Roman
     Bold
     Light

     Style.
     Regular
     Sloping

  ii) Depict the mood of the story.
     Use of words
     Selection of font style

  iii) Set the tone of the newspaper.
     Point size
     Headline style

  iv) Provide typographical relief.
     Contrast: Light/Bold/Italics
     Separate stories: Light/Bold

2

HOW TO WRITE A HEADLINE

Headline writing is a craft, and like any other craft needs to be learnt the hard way. To use an oft-repeated cliché, a good headline is the outcome of 99 per cent perspiration and 1 per cent inspiration. The best method is to adopt a step-by-step approach, to define each parameter carefully, and then to narrow down possibilities to one good, finely chiselled headline.

STEP 1: LOCATE THE NEWS POINT

A headline writer must first decide the news point on which a story rests. This is not a very difficult task since 90 per cent of news reports are written in the inverted pyramid format. In this format, a reporter builds the news lead on the most important news point. The remaining news points follow in decreasing order of importance. The headline writer therefore does not have to dig very deep to write the headline. In nine out of 10 reports the news point will be available in the lead paragraph itself.

Given below are two leads that were built on the news point. The first lead highlights a boat tragedy in which 20 people were feared dead; the second speaks about a meeting between the foreign ministers of India and Pakistan.

The second lead provides two news points on which the headline can be written. The first is the straight headline that announces a meeting between the two foreign ministers; the second highlights the issues that are likely to figure in the meeting. The second headline is the better of the two since it informs the reader of what is likely to happen during the meeting.

Lead 1
JAUNPUR, (UNI): At least 20 people were feared dead after a boat ferrying devotees capsized in river Gomti under Chandwak police circle here this morning.
Headline:
20 feared dead in UP boat mishap

Lead 2
ISLAMABAD (IANS): India's External Affairs Minister K. Natwar Singh and his

Headline Writing

Pakistani counterpart Khurshid Mehmood Kasuri will meet here on Wednesday to discuss the bilateral peace process, including the Kashmir issue.

Headlines

Natwar Singh, Kasuri to meet on Wednesday
India, Pak foreign ministers to meet on Wednesday
Natwar, Kasuri to discuss Kashmir, bilateral issues

However, there are stories, especially feature or analytical stories, where the news point may be buried deep in the report. In such cases, the headline writer has to locate the news point by reading the report carefully.

Step 2: Decide Display

The display of a news report depends on three factors:
  (*a*) importance,
  (*b*) relative importance as compared to other reports on the page, and
  (*c*) length.

The first two factors are intertwined and depend upon the news assessment skills of the headline writer. For example, let us look at a story that reports the death of 20 persons in a boat accident in Lucknow. A newspaper published from Lucknow would certainly run the report as the lead story of the day since it is a local tragedy. The report, however, may not be the lead story in a newspaper published from New Delhi because there may be other national events that may vie for the lead spot. But since Lucknow is a state capital the report can get a multicolumn display on the front page.

However, a newspaper printed from Chennai will not accord the tragedy the same priority as the Lucknow or Delhi newspaper. It will in all probability run it as a single column story. Even this single column display will depend upon the importance of the Lucknow story vis-à-vis other stories on the page.

Let us assume a scenario where the Uttar Pradesh government was dismissed on the day the boat tragedy occurred. Will the boat tragedy still be displayed as the lead story in the Lucknow newspaper? No. The lead story will be the dismissal of the UP government since it is an event of a much larger magnitude. The boat story will then get a multicolumn display lower down on the page. The Delhi newspaper will scale down the boat tragedy display to a single column while the Chennai newspaper may push it to an inside page. This is what is meant by display being decided by the relative importance of a news story.

The headline writer cannot overlook the length of the story in deciding the display. If the Lucknow bureau of a Delhi newspaper files only two paragraphs on the boat tragedy, then the Delhi newspaper cannot give it a multicolumn display. The story will have to be run as a single column since it lacks sufficient depth to be spread across two, three or four columns. The second step therefore in writing a headline is to decide the display—the number of columns across which a story is to be run.

STEP 3: DECIDE POINT SIZE AND STYLE

The headline point size and style depend upon three factors:
(a) column width,
(b) design needs, and
(c) nature of the story.

Quite clearly, a small point size will be used to write a headline that is to be run in a single column and a large point size for headlines that are to be run across multicolumns. The largest point size will be reserved for the lead story.

Sometimes a large point size may be used for a headline written in a single column, especially if the story is run on top of the page. Such decisions are based on design needs and are taken to make the page visually pleasing.

The typestyle depends on the nature of the story. A bold typeface will be used for hard news headlines and a light or italics typeface will be used for offbeat stories.

The design editor in consultation with the editor and the publisher selects the headline font or typeface, headline typestyle and headline point sizes. This is done to ensure uniformity in selection of headline point sizes and typefaces. Good newspapers insist that the news desk follow these guidelines faithfully.

The importance of such a style guide (Fig. 2.1) cannot be overstressed, especially in today s work cnvironment where desktop publishing has made it possible to write headlines in a multitude of typefaces, type sizes and typestyles. There is also the added possibility of kerning, expanding or condensing headlines. These variations, however, destroy the homogeneity of a news page and must be banned in any good newsroom.

Headline style guide	
Type face	Times New Roman
Type style	Roman, Bold, Italics
Point sizes	
Single column	14, 16, 18
Double column	28, 32, 36
Three columns and above: Single line	32, 36, 40
Three columns and above: Double line	32
Lead	48
Anchor	36
Shoulder/Kicker	14
Reverse shoulder/Strapline	20

Fig. 2.1: *The prototype of a headline style chart.*

Based on the importance of the story and the column display, the headline writer will select a point size and style specified by the design editor.

STEP 4: DECIDE THE NUMBER OF DECKS OR LINES

There is one more decision that the headline writer needs to take before writing the headline, and that is deciding the number of decks. The number of decks or lines depends on two main factors: (*a*) length of the story and (*b*) design needs.

Newspapers generally frown upon a multideck display for headlines written in three or more columns. This is because a double deck headline for a four-column story looks too heavy on a page. In the case of five or more columns such a display will look positively ugly. That is why a double deck headline is largely used for double column displays and very rarely beyond that.

In the case of single columns, the standard practice is to use three decks unless the story is short. Four decks are used only when the story is very important or the headline is to be used as a design tool.

STEP 5: IDENTIFY KEYWORDS

The traditional news lead is built around the five 'Ws' and an 'H'. Since the headline cannot use all the six elements — there is not enough space to do so — it uses the most important Ws to convey the essence of a report. The 'Ws' so chosen are called keywords. Invariably they comprise the subject, which is a noun, and the action taken by the subject, which is expressed by a verb or a verb phrase. The other parts of speech are put in to add value to the headline.

Let us identify keywords in the following lead:

LUCKNOW (IANS): It sounds unbelievable, but hundreds of men in Uttar Pradesh have been literally buying brides for just Rs 5,000. And the men of Jalaun district of southern Uttar Pradesh do not have to go farther than Nagpur in Maharashtra, where poverty-stricken parents happily hand over their daughters for a price.

The five Ws and an H in the above lead are:
Who: UP's men
What: Buying brides
Where: Nagpur
How: By paying Rs 5,000
When: Continuing process
Why: Easy

The keywords for this story therefore are:
UP's men
Buying brides
Nagpur

By paying Rs 5,000
Continuing process
Easy

STEP 6: WRITE THE FIRST HEADLINE

Having identified the keywords, the headline writer needs to decide which Ws are most important. The first W clearly is Who; without this W the headline will be incomplete. Therefore the first keyword to be used in the headline is 'UP's men'. The second W is what are they doing. The answer to this is sensational: they are buying brides. Therefore the next keyword to be used is 'buying brides'. The third W gives the name of the city from where the brides are being bought—'Nagpur'. The fourth important W is the price, which is Rs 5,000. The fifth and sixth Ws are not so important. They provide generalized information. The headline, if it is to accommodate the first four Ws, will read:

UP's men buying brides from Nagpur for Rs 5,000

STEP 7: POLISH THE HEADLINE

The first priority after writing the rough headline should be to correct the syntax or the sentence structure. In this headline, the price of the brides comes in the end; it should be moved forward and brought next to the noun brides.

UP's men buying brides for Rs 5,000 from Nagpur

The noun men is too vague. It should be turned into a concrete noun. Since the story is about marriages for a price, the word 'men' can be substituted with 'grooms' or 'bachelors'.

UP's grooms buy brides for Rs 5,000 from Nagpur
UP's bachelors buy brides for Rs 5,000 from Nagpur

HEADLINES FOR MULTIPLE-POINT LEADS

The difficulty arises when a news lead is made of multiple points. In the following report moved by DPA from Singapore there were two key points. The first was that a Singapore employer had not paid salaries to 40 Indian workers for periods ranging from three to six months. The second point spoke about the reaction of Indian workers—that they were asking Singaporean companies to give them food for work till their employer cleared their dues. Both the points were important.

News Lead

SINGAPORE (DPA): Forty foreign workers from India claim they have not been paid for six months and have been knocking on doors seeking work in exchange for food, news reports said on Monday. Sleeping in a shabby unit of a shophouse, the workers refuse to return to their homeland without the money due to them.

The five Ws and an H in the lead are:
Who: 40 Indian workers
What: Seeking food for work
Where: Singapore
When: Not clear
Why: Not paid for six months
How: Knocking at company doors

The keywords for this story therefore are:
40 Indian workers
Singapore company
No salary for 6 months
Food in lieu of work

The headline can be:

40 Indians not paid for 6 months in Singapore

or

40 Indians seek food in lieu of work in Singapore

or

The writer can combine the two points to write a single headline.

40 Indians seek food in lieu of work in Singapore as employer refuses to pay

The second headline captures the main points in the story much better. However, in doing so it ends up using more space, necessitating a multicolumn or multideck display. This is not always possible as multicolumn display is related to several factors like the importance and depth of a story and page design.

HEADLINE COUNT: A REDUNDANT STEP NOW

The first step in headline writing in the pre-desktop publishing era was mastering the headline counting system. Unlike today, it was not possible to kern or condense headlines. The typefaces were made of metal and mounted on wood. They were then placed in metal frames, which left no space to squeeze extra letters if the headline overshot the column width. A fresh headline had to be written and composed for even one extra letter. This involved a considerable waste of time since the headline had to be reset — a practice that no press foreman liked.

The news desk was therefore required to count each letter in the headline before sending it to the press. The counting was based on simple logic. Letters that occupied uniform space like 'a' or 'c' were counted as one while letters that took relatively more space like 'w' and 'm' were counted as one and a half; small 'i' or small 'l' were counted as half. There was a different count for headlines set in all capitals; thus capital 'W' and 'M' were counted as two. There was a count for punctuation marks as well as for space between words.

A headline count key was kept on all news desks enabling the headline writer to know how many letters could be accommodated in single column setting in different point sizes. Based on this, the headline writer could work out the letter count for multicolumn headlines. A headline was rejected if it overshot this count by even one point. The subeditor had to write a fresh headline. This discipline made headline writing a great craft.

It is a pity that the desktop publishing system has eliminated this great practice altogether. Now a subeditor writes a headline and leaves the counting to the computer. In case the headline is long, the writer tries short cuts like removing words or even condensing alphabets and lets the computer do the rest. The thought that went into headline writing in the earlier era is gone. Today fitting the headline in a column is more by trial and error. As a desk man who has worked both in the hot metal and the desktop printing era, I have no hesitation in advocating the need to teach the headline counting system even today. It is still a very useful tool and must be taught to all budding journalists, both in journalism schools and in newsrooms.

There were two different counts; one for headlines written in the upper-lower format and the other for headlines written in all capitals. The count in each format is given in Fig. 2.2:

Upper-lower system

Letters	Count
1. All lowercase letters with exception of seven letters	1
2. i, j, f, t, l	0.5
3. m, w	1.5
4. All capital letters with the exception of two letters	1.5
5. M, W	2
6. Numerals	1
7. Space between words	1
8. Punctuation marks with two exceptions	0.5
9. ? and !	1

All capitals headline

Letters	Count
1. All letters with the exception of two	1
2. M, W	1.5
3. Numerals	1
4. Space between words	1
5. Punctuation marks with two exceptions	0.5
6. ? and !	1

Fig. 2.2: *The headline counting guide that gives the count for each letter.*

CHAPTER HIGHLIGHTS

The seven steps to write a headline

1. Locate the news point.
2. Decide display.
3. Decide point size and style.
4. Decide number of decks.
5. Identify keywords.
6. Write the first headline.
7. Polish the headline.

Where can the news point be found

1. In the lead paragraph of news reports written in the inverted pyramid format.
2. In the body of analytical, feature or descriptive stories.

How to decide display

1. Assess the importance of the news report.
2. Assess the relative importance of the news report.
3. Check the length of the report.

How to decide point size and style

1. Base it on column width chosen to display the story.
2. Weigh design needs to provide contrast and balance.
3. Bring out the nature of the story, especially if it is a soft or offbeat story.

How to decide the number of decks

1. Check the story length.
2. Use multiple decks for long stories.
3. Weigh design needs to provide contrast and balance.

How to identify keywords

1. List the five Ws and the H.
2. Decide which of them is more relevant.
3. Select the subject.
4. Select the most important action.
5. Build the headline around the subject and the action taken.

HEADLINE EXERCISE

Ten news reports filed by UNI and PTI are listed below. Please write a headline for each using the seven steps listed in this chapter and as shown in the example below. The eighth step—that of headline count—may have become redundant but it is essential for this exercise. Please count the letters after writing the headline to ensure that it will fit. The typeface, column width and headline count is given in the first exercise. Please follow the instructions carefully and write the headline in the same manner as has been done for the Tiruchirappali report.

Instructors are welcome to change the point size or column width. However, it is essential that they insist on headline count. This will help students learn to write headlines that will fit in the given space in the newspaper.

> TIRUCHIRAPALLI (UNI) : A 41-year-old person committed suicide near the "navagraha sannidhi" of the historic Sri Jambukeswara-Akhilandeswari Temple at Tiruvanaikoil here last evening.
>
> Police said Jambulingam, an employee of the temple, used to take contract for the sale of small clay lamps inside the temple complex.
>
> This year he reportedly lost the contract during the auction.
>
> Pained over this and unable to bear mounting debts, he hung himself in the temple premises.

Headline parameters
Point size: 16
Case: Upper-lower
Number of letters per column: 18
Column width: One
Number of decks: Three

Step 1
Locate news point.
Man hangs himself to death in Trichy temple

Step 2
Decide display.
Single column

Step 3
Decide point size.
16 upper-lower

Step 4
Decide number of decks.
Three

Step 5

Locate keywords.

Who: Contractor
What: Commits suicide
Where: Trichy temple
When: Yesterday
Why: Did not get contract
How: By hanging

First draft of the headline

Contractor hangs	15.5
himself in	8.5
Trichy temple	12.5

The headline conveys the main news point as per the point size and display decided for the news report. However, the second deck is much smaller than the first one; there is space to squeeze in more words. The third deck too can accommodate a few more characters.

The headline should be revised to give the reason for the suicide. This added description makes the headline complete; also, it makes the three decks fuller, which is an important design requirement for any good headline.

Revised/polished headline

Man loses contract,	17.5
hangs himself	14
in Trichy temple	15

Exercise 1

MORADABAD (UNI): Special Operation Group (SOG) sleuths of the Uttar Pradesh Police have seized 10 kg opium worth Rs five lakh with the arrest of a head constable's son.

SOG sources said here today the sleuths intercepted a motorcycle near Fawwara Chowk here last evening. On frisking, the cops recovered 10 kg opium from the duo.

They were later arrested. One of them was identified as Rajesh alias Bharat, son of a head constable.

Headline parameters

Point size: 16
Case: Upper-lower
Number of letters per column: 18
Column width: One
Number of decks: Three

Step 1
Locate news point.

Step 2
Decide display.

Step 3
Decide point size.

Step 4
Decide number of decks.

Step 5
Locate keywords.
Who:
What:
Where:
When:
Why:
How:

Step 6
First Headline   <u>Count</u>

Step 7
Polish the headline.

Exercise 2

BAREILLY (UNI): Nine inmates of a juvenile home escaped last night after attacking its caretaker and guard in this district of Uttar Pradesh.

The Senior Superintendent of Police said the warden of the juvenile home, located in the Rampur Garden area, had reportedly locked the children in a room after serving them dinner. Later, one of the inmates called the guard and when he opened the door, another inmate attacked him with a knife and snatched the keys.

The nine later opened the doors and fled.

Exercise 3

NEW DELHI (UNI): The Kingfisher is set to fly with Bangalore-based liquor czar Vijay Mallya getting ready to launch a low-cost carrier by this year-end.

His UB group is already involved in aviation as a non-scheduled operator with a charter permit. Next week, it will file application for scheduled operations across the country.

"We are evaluating various options for the type of aircraft to use but in our application, we will file for Airbus A-320 with 150 to 179 passenger seats," Mr Mallya said.

Exercise 4

KANCHEEPURAM (UNI): In a tragic accident, six persons, including a woman, were charred to death and 21 injured seriously when a private bus collided head-on with a lorry early this morning near Sriperumbudur on the Chennai-Bangalore National Highway.

Police said both the vehicles caught fire immediately after the collision. While three persons, including the woman, died on the spot, three others were rushed to the Kilpauk Medical College Hospital at Chennai where they succumbed to death.

Exercise 5

BAREILLY (UNI): A police inspector and two constables were allegedly beaten up and their arms snatched by the residents of the Bhimpur village in this district of Uttar Pradesh when they went there to seize hooch.

Police said the incident occurred last night at around 2300 hrs when a police team led by an inspector raided various places in the village to seize the illicit liquor.

Later, senior police officials rushed to the site and admitted the injured policemen to a public health centre in Aonla area. The arms of the policemen taken away by the villagers were yet to be recovered. As many as 20 people have so far died after drinking hooch in the district during the past five days.

Exercise 6

NEW DELHI (UNI): Having proposed a strategic partnership with India, the European Union says it is keen to upgrade relations with India to a level that supersedes even that it has with China.

"Our ambition is to take our relations with India even higher than what we have with China," Mr Francisco da Camara Gomes, Ambassador, Head of the Delegation of European Commission in India, said at an interactive session with the Forum of Financial Writers.

A communication last week by the European Commission set out proposals for upgrading ties with India to a strategic partnership. However, Mr Gomes indicated that the EU's aim was not to stop here, but take the India-EU relations on a much higher plane.

Exercise 7

NEW DELHI (UNI): With new chic, sleek cars widening the choice of buyers almost every year, the used car market in the country has also started growing as more and more people from the upper strata are rejecting their old vehicles in favour of the new beauties.

These rejections find their way into the homes of middle and lower middle classes. The bargain is not bad for them if they can find a two or three year old Maruti 800, a Zen or a Santro or an Indica in almost "as good as new" condition for a price lower by a lakh.

The demand is not only for small cars, but also for the big ones, as those who can afford to buy a new small car prefer to buy a used big car in a good condition to enjoy its added comforts at a price they would pay for a smaller car, or just for the sake of the status symbol attached with these plush objects.

Exercise 8

PATNA (IANS): A rare freshwater Gangetic dolphin that had got entangled in the fishing nets was let off into the river Ganges in Bihar after being rescued from fishermen.

The Zoological Survey of India in-charge, Gopal Sharma, said the dolphin weighing 10 kg was released near the confluence of the rivers Ganges and Gandak here.

The Ganges in Bihar has the largest surviving population of this dolphin species.

Dolphins are mainly hunted in the summer when they congregate at the confluence of the Ganga and Gandak to find food.

Exercise 9

KUMBAKONAM (PTI): In a grand finale to the ten-day Mahamaham festival in Kumbakonam, in Tamil Nadu, about 20 lakh devotees from across the country took a holy dip and offered special poojas, to invoke the blessings of Lord Shiva and Vishnu at the famous Mahamaham tank and Chakratheertham on Saturday.

The devotees who began thronging the tank since Feb 26, when the Mahamaham festival began, were allowed in batches of 30,000 at a time to the tank, and each batch was given five minutes to finish their poojas and take holy bath, police said.

Exercise 10

PATNA (IANS): For the first time in hundreds of years, a temple in a Bihar town will not offer traditional animal sacrifices on Durga Puja this year following a ban by local authorities.

Priests at the Shaktipeeth Maa Chandika temple in Munger decided not to follow the age-old practice after the district magistrate ordered a ban on animal slaughter.

"For the first time, sacrifices will not be offered to the goddess," a temple priest said. Hundreds of animals used to be sacrificed every year during Durga Puja at this temple.

3 | KINDS OF HEADLINES – I

LABEL HEADLINE

A headline that lacks a verb is referred to as a label headline. Such a headline does not convey the action taken by the subject. Instead it limits itself to the subject only. Look at the following two examples of label headlines:

KSRTC fares
Car sales

Both the headlines are silent on the action taken. The reader needs to go through the story to learn if the KSRTC fares have increased or car sales have declined.

Generally, label headlines are used for reports where the headline writer is constrained for space like the front-page briefs or city briefs (Fig. 3.1). These headlines are incomplete and play a very perfunctory role. They evoke scorn when used with hard news reports (Fig. 3.2). Yet, headline writers when pressed for time slap label headlines and release pages.

Fig. 3.1: *Label headlines written for news reports used in city briefs.*

Writers, theatre artistes for Kannada movies

BY OUR CORRESPONDENT	ous release of non Kannada films in the state.	immediate attention to solve the crisis in the film industry.	parochial and chauvinistic. Kasaravalli said the Kannada	Kannada films are fighting with the best films of six na
Bangalore, Sept. 22: Several Kannada literary, theatre and	The personalities who include award-winning films	They termed the agitation of the Kannada film industry on	film industry was passing through one crisis after	Kannada languages. It is al wrong to say that Kannada

Fig. 3.2: *A label headline used with a hard news story in the* Asian Age.

Label headlines are also found in advertisement supplements published to promote companies or commercial activities. This is because marketing teams that handle supplements are unfamiliar with headline writing techniques.

DESCRIPTIVE HEADLINES

Headlines that speak the loudest are descriptive headlines, and the newspaper that should be credited for pioneering this genre of headline writing in India is the *Asian Age*. Initially, descriptive headlines bred scepticism, but gradually most newspapers started switching to the descriptive format. These go beyond the simple noun and the verb; they capture the essence of the stories graphically. Some of the characteristics of descriptive headlines are discussed below:

Capture a Story's Essence

In the Taj Corridor scam, the Supreme Court in 2003 ordered the Central Bureau of Investigation (CBI), to step up investigations against four government officials. The order was based on a preliminary report submitted by the investigating agency and did not reveal the names of officials. The *Hindu* ran a straight and traditional headline:

SC directive to CBI on Taj

The headline performed the most perfunctory of tasks. It informed the reader that the Supreme Court had given an order to the CBI. To know what this order was or how it would impact on the investigation, the reader needed to go through the story.

The New Delhi Television Ltd (NDTV) website carried this functionality a little further. It fleshed out the headline by stating:

Probe UP officials linked to Taj Corridor: SC

The *Times of India* captured the essence of the Supreme Court directive when it wrote:

SC to CBI: Grill big fish in Taj mess

A similar sentiment was conveyed in the *Indian Express* headline. The *Express* also stressed the urgency of the Supreme Court directive by stating that the court wanted the CBI to finish its investigation quickly.

SC tells CBI to go after the Taj 'high & mighty', get back fast

The extra description adds value to the headline. The readers, like the television viewers, instantly comprehend the main point of the story. They may now choose to go through the story or not but the headline has achieved its first objective: of conveying the main point of the story.

Provide Extra Information

Fugitives use innovative ways to frustrate the law. One such story was of an Indian who swallowed a knife to avoid extradition from Germany. There were three headlines that were written for the following story:

> NEW DELHI: Amarendra Nath Ghosh, who was on the verge of being extradited to India in a bank fraud case by the CBI, has swallowed a knife in Germany in a desperate bid to delay the inevitable.
>
> (para 3) However, when the CBI was about to send its team to Germany to bring him back here, the CBI got an urgent message from the German authorities asking the agency team to hold on as 'Ghosh had swallowed an eight centimetre knife and badly hurt himself.'

Headline 1: **Fugitive swallows knife to avoid extradition**
Headline 2: **Indian swallows knife to avoid extradition**
Headline 3: **Indian swallows 8 cm knife to avoid extradition**

Headline 1 spoke of a fugitive, who could be of any nationality. Headline 2 removed this ambiguity by using the concrete word 'Indian'. This headline would have aroused relatively more interest in India because an Indian was involved. Headline 3 added one critical fact—the size of the knife. The headline now had both drama and description; it was complete.

This is the second major attribute that any good headline should have. It should delve deep into the story and locate interesting nuggets to make the headline grab attention.

Remove Ambiguity

The best descriptive headlines are those that use familiar and concrete words. They evoke reader interest by highlighting facts and use words that a reader can comprehend or relate to.

A recent addition to the English language is the term 'road rage'. It is used to describe acts of violence committed by frustrated and angry drivers, often on flimsy pretexts. One incident that sparked outrage in Delhi involved a Russian and an Indian couple. According to reports, the Russian's car hit the businessman's car near Chanakyapuri, Delhi's high profile diplomatic area, one Sunday. The Russian is then reported to have jumped out and used an iron bar to smash the businessman's car window in anger. When the businessman tried to reason, he and his wife were beaten by the Russian.

The headline made a simple statement of fact:

Russian involved in road rage in Delhi

The headline was not wrong, but it was bland. There was no description of the incident. Instead, a broad term 'road rage' was used to describe it. It was left to the reader to read the story and find out what happened. Was it a heated exchange of words, a blocking of vehicles, a minor scuffle or physical violence?

The headline writer needed to liven up the headline by describing what had happened as has been done in this revised headline.

Road rage in Delhi: Russian beats up Indian couple, smashes car

Another report to which the headline writer failed to do justice was a UNI story that was moved from Dubai. The first three paragraphs of the story were as follows:

> DUBAI (UNI): The humiliating and degrading treatment, including shaving the heads of Indian expatriate workers by overzealous Saudi authorities trying to enforce the government's Saudization orders, has come in for condemnation in the Kingdom's media.
>
> The influential Jeddah-based *Arab News* described the tonsuring of ticketing clerks after raids on travel agencies as "appalling and sad because it happened in Saudi Arabia, the birthplace of Islam, the protector of all human rights".
>
> Implementation of Saudization rules is one thing; Saudization is the law and the law must not be ignored. But dragging off ticketing clerks and shaving their heads is quite another, the paper said in an editorial on Thursday.

The headline writer preferred the broad term 'humiliated' to bring out the suffering of the Indians.

Indian workers humiliated in Saudi Arabia

It did not highlight the fact that Indians were physically dragged or their heads tonsured as this revised headline does.

Saudis drag Indian workers, tonsure them

Add Drama and Colour

Another important characteristic of descriptive headlines is that they use adjectives and adverbs to spruce up, and add spice to, the message. However, this needs great skill since unnecessary or excessive use of adjectives or adverbs will make the headline look amateurish.

For instance, the campaign demanding a ban on cow slaughter was high voltage stuff. For months, the nation was lectured on the merits of banning cow slaughter; the beef eaters were equally vocal in putting forth their point of view. The battle peaked when the bill came to the voting stage in 2003. However, before this could happen the then National Democratic Alliance (NDA) government announced that the cow slaughter bill was being put on hold.

The essence of the story was best captured in this lead run in the *Indian Express*.

NEW DELHI: Angry NDA members and allies on Thursday forced the Government to put on hold the controversial Bill banning cow slaughter across the country. But the BJP, keen on pushing the Bill ahead of the Assembly elections, took heart from the fact that the message had gone out: the move to bring in a law against cow slaughter was being opposed by other parties.

It is interesting to note how the headline writers captured the drama. Four headlines that deserve mention for the story are:

Straight headline: **Govt defers Bill banning cow slaughter**

Comment: **Allies force govt to defer Bill banning cow slaughter**

Smart turn of phrase: **Allies make BJP climb down the cow**

Comment plus description: **Snorting allies force Govt to tether Cow Bill**

The first two are functional headlines while the last two reflect the headline writer's creativity. The use of the words 'snorting' and 'tether' is certainly praiseworthy.

Need More Space

The only negative characteristic of descriptive headlines is that they need more space since they use extra words. This may not always be possible in a newspaper where space is at a premium. Headline writers need to select words carefully when writing a descriptive headline. Otherwise, they need to use headline props (see Chapter 5).

HEADLINING A RUNNING STORY

Three points must be kept in mind while writing a headline for a running story. These are:

Focus on the Latest Development

This will spark the readers' curiosity and interest. Headlines that attempt to refresh the readers' memory as to what happened yesterday waste space and readers' time.

It is the current day's development that matters and the headline writers must focus on it.

A headline that was way off the mark was the one written for the killing of a railway engineer and his brother in Kashmir. The story had grabbed national attention ever since the abduction took place. However, the headline writer chose to stress the kidnapping more than the killing in the headline even after the bodies of the brothers had been recovered.

> PULWAMA: Targeting the Qazigund-Baramulla railway project for the first time, suspected militants on Friday executed a railway engineer and his 18-year-old brother on Friday after keeping them in captivity for two days.

Headline used: **IRCON engineer, brother kidnapped, butchered**
Quite clearly the focus was wrong. The development was the recovery of the bodies. A more appropriate headline would have been:

Captors kill abducted IRCON engineer, brother
or

Bodies of kidnapped rail engineer, brother found

Use a Word or Phrase that Works as a Connecting Thread

The headline of a running story needs a connecting thread. This thread can be any word or phrase that best symbolizes the story. For instance, the sharing of Cauvery waters has become a major bone of contention between Karnataka and Tamil Nadu. The issue invariably flares up around July every year with Tamil Nadu demanding the release of the agreed share of Cauvery waters and Karnataka reluctant to do so on grounds that there is not enough water in the river.

There is a flurry of stories with statements made by leaders of the two states; inspections by neutral advisers; appeals to the prime minister to resolve the issue; even filing of cases before the Supreme Court by the two states to secure their rights. It therefore makes sense to use a link word or phrase to connect the flood of stories on the subject. This link word or phrase can be: Cauvery waters, Cauvery issue or Cauvery dispute.

Newspapers have evolved different ways to display the link word or link phrase (see Chapter 5). The most common one is to use the link phrase as the story's shoulder or kicker. When violence flared up in Mumbai's King Edward Memorial hospital and the patients attacked doctors, the *Indian Express* used the link phrase 'Attack on Doctors' to connect the running story (Fig. 3.3).

Another way is to place the link word in the strapline as has been popularized by the *Indian Express*. During the run up to the 2004 Assembly elections in Maharashtra the link words 'Assembly Polls 2004' were used in the strapline (Fig. 3.4).

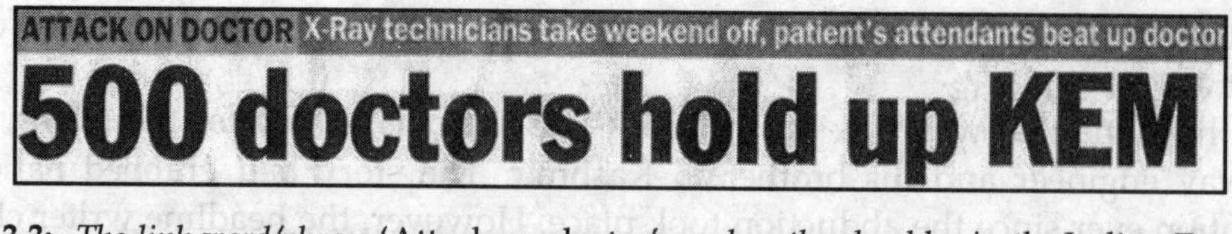

64

Fig. 3.3: *The link word/phrase* 'Attack on doctor' *used as the shoulder in the* Indian Express.

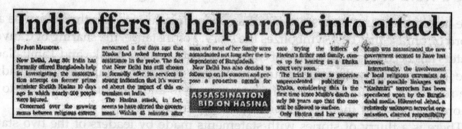

Fig. 3.4: The *link word/phrase* 'Assembly Polls 2004' *used in the strapline in the* Indian Express.

A third way is to place the link words as a navigation aid in the middle of the story. For instance, the *New Indian Express* used the subject line 'Assassination bid on Hasina' in the middle of the running story (Fig. 3.5). This enabled the reader to learn the developments related to the assassination bid on former Prime Minister of Bangladesh, Ms Sheikh Hasina, in August 2004.

Fig. 3.5: *The subject line* 'Assassination bid on Hasina' *used in the middle of the story as a connecting thread in the* New Indian Express.

In all the three methods, the headline writers are not constrained by the link phrase when it comes to writing the main headline. They can use the entire headline width to focus on the day's developments and provide more information. This does not mean that the link phrase should not be used as part of the main headline. It can be used as long as it allows the headline writers to highlight the day's developments effectively.

HEADLINES FOR MULTIPLE-POINT LEADS

All stories are not built around a single point. There are several events, such as sensational kidnappings, terror killings or coalition squabbles, which need a more comprehensive coverage especially if they happen to be running stories.

The headline writers, of course, have the option to select the news point which in their opinion is the most important, and build a headline around it. But in doing so they may ignore several equally important and competing points. It is therefore advisable to use straplines or link words when confronted with a multiple point story (see also Chapter 5).

Procedure to be Followed

The following procedure needs to be adopted while writing the headline for a multiple-point story:

i)   Select the most important point.
ii) Write the main headline on this point.
iii) Select the second most important point.
iv) Use a strapline to convey this point.
v)   Use a link word in the strapline or in the middle of the report if it is a running story.

In 2003, India boycotted an International Conference on Terrorism that was organized by the United Nations in New York. India's strong reaction followed a speech by President Pervez Musharraf of Pakistan who accused India of carrying out state sponsored terrorism in Kashmir. India's Foreign Secretary, Mr Kanwal Sibal, who briefed the press on India's decision was scathing. The main point of the story, of course, was India's decision to stay away from the conference, and this went to make the headline. The strapline used a juicy byte from the statement made by Mr Sibal. The strapline also used the link words 'PM at UN' since this was a running story as the prime minister was in New York to attend the annual meeting of the United Nations General Assembly.

Main Headline: **India skips meet after Gen utters K-word**
Strapline with link words: **PM AT UN Pak's Kashmir itch rules out talks; they should fast before coming to UN: Sibal**

Cause and Effect

There are some news reports where the cause is as important as the effect. It therefore pays to highlight both the points in the headline. For instance, the US Deputy Secretary of State Richard Armitage's visit to India in July 2004 coincided with a controversy about the reported body search of the former Minister of Defence George Fernandes by the US customs.

Clearly, the American officials did not want Mr Armitage's visit to be clouded by the row. They therefore chose to issue an official apology on the eve of Mr Armitage's arrival. The *Indian Express* reporter who wrote the story captured this point brilliantly in the lead; and the headline writer did justice to the lead by highlighting the apology's 'cause-and-effect' relationship. The newspaper's lead, which follows, was an example of good journalism.

NEW DELHI: Seeking to calm the ripples on the reported "strip-search" of former Defence Minister George Fernandes at a US airport in 2003, and on the eve of US Deputy Secretary Richard Armitage's talks with the senior Indian leadership on Wednesday, the US Embassy here apologised on Tuesday.

On eve of Armitage's talks, US says sorry to George

The headline would have lost impact if it had been limited to the apology alone, which incidentally was a major news point since senior government officials do not apologize for past faux pas every day. The headline brought out the apology's motive.

Figurative Usage

Sometimes the lead is crammed with three or even more points, each equally important. A good way to write headlines for such multipoint leads is to use figurative headlines.

Two brilliant figurative headlines were written—one by the *Hindustan Times* and the other by the *Indian Express*—when the Minister of Agriculture, Mr Sharad Pawar, lost the election for the post of the President, Board of Control for Cricket in India. It was an election that had the whole of India transfixed. There was suspense, drama and intrigue.

Both the newspapers used cricket imagery to write the headlines. The *Indian Express* used a strapline to support the main headline (Fig. 3.6); the *Hindustan Times* used decks to capture the important points of that eventful election (Fig. 3.7). The headline would have been incomplete if the following points were not captured, either directly or by implication:
  i)   defeat of Sharad Pawar;
  ii) election of Ranbir Singh Mahendra as BCCI Chief;
  iii) clever poll management by Jagmohan Dalmiya; and
  iv) reaction of Pawar at the loss.

The *Indian Express* headline

Main headline:	**Pawar st Ranbir b Dalmiya**
Strapline:	**BCCI ELECTIONS: Bowler and umpire same person, fumes Maratha satrap after stunning loss**

The *Hindustan Times* headline

Main Headline:	**Dalmiya wins tied match**
First deck:	**Pawar says he got out to bad decision**
Second deck:	**Ranbir Singh new BCCI Chief**

Fig. 3.6: *The headline used by the* Indian Express *for the report on the eventful election to the post of President, Board of Control for Cricket in India.*

Fig. 3.7: *The deck format used by the* Hindustan Times *for the BCCI President's election.*

COMMENTATIVE HEADLINES

A recent trend in headline writing in India is the injection of comments in headlines. This is largely a result of interpretative reporting that is increasingly becoming a part of Indian newspapers. These reports analyse the implications of a news development or look behind the scenes in an effort to provide something extra to their readers. The liberal use of comment in these news reports has now started reflecting in headlines too.

The row over awarding of cricket telecast rights in 2004 witnessed a flurry of activity. There was a spate of statements involving the three key players—Board of Control for Cricket in India, Zee TV and ESPN-Star Sports. The following is a headline used for a story on the row run in the *Asian Age*:

**Desperate Dalmiya wants
to sabotage clean Zee bid**

This was a strong headline as it commented on the BCCI official who was the key person in deciding the awarding of telecast rights (Fig. 3.8). The official was accused of using desperate methods to sabotage Zee's bid that the headline asserted was clean.

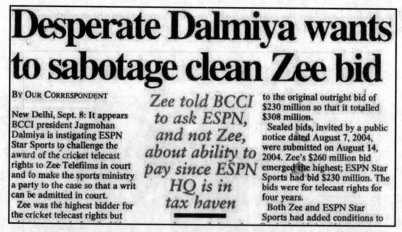

Desperate Dalmiya wants to sabotage clean Zee bid

BY OUR CORRESPONDENT

New Delhi, Sept. 8: It appears BCCI president Jagmohan Dalmiya is instigating ESPN Star Sports to challenge the award of the cricket telecast rights to Zee Telefilms in court and to make the sports ministry a party to the case so that a writ can be admitted in court.

Zee was the highest bidder for the cricket telecast rights but

Zee told BCCI to ask ESPN, and not Zee, about ability to pay since ESPN HQ is in tax haven

to the original outright bid of $230 million so that it totalled $308 million.

Sealed bids, invited by a public notice dated August 7, 2004, were submitted on August 14, 2004. Zee's $260 million bid emerged the highest; ESPN Star Sports had bid $230 million. The bids were for telecast rights for four years.

Both Zee and ESPN Star Sports had added conditions to

Fig. 3.8: *The commentative headline used by the* Asian Age *during the telecast rights' row.*

There is little doubt that the trend of using comment in headlines will grow in the coming years. Comment certainly adds colour to a headline. But headline writers need to be careful when introducing comment. They must remember that comment is a two-edged sword; if used wrongly, it can lead to legal trouble.

They need to weigh the advantages and dangers of comment before using it in headlines.

Add Extra Meaning to a Headline

This is especially true of stories where a reporter analyses the implications of a development. A good example of this was the visit of the Prime Minister of Israel, Mr Ariel Sharon, to India. The visit was a major shift in foreign policy and there were fears of a negative reaction in the Arab world. Interestingly, the Indian Foreign Office scheduled a visit by a Palestinian delegation days before Mr Sharon's arrival. It is difficult to say whether this was a conscious move on the part of New Delhi or accidental.

Two headlines written for the story make interesting reading. The first merely mentioned the fact that New Delhi had invited Palestinians ahead of Mr Sharon. Headline 1 was loaded with meaning but it was left to the reader to decipher it. Headline 2 was bolder. It announced that the two visits were New Delhi's way to balance the Sharon visit.

Headline 1: **New Delhi invites Palestinians ahead of Sharon**
Headline 2: **New Delhi's balancing act: Ahead of Sharon trip, Palestinians invited**

Another good commentative headline was used for the resignation story of Mr Shibu Soren, a Union Minister, who fled Delhi when the Jharkhand police came to arrest him. The opposition National Democratic Alliance (NDA) mounted a fierce campaign seeking Mr Soren's resignation. The Congress-led United Progressive Alliance (UPA) government dithered for some time as Mr Soren's party was an important member of the coalition. The Prime Minister finally had to bow to opposition pressure and seek Mr Soren's resignation. All parties were therefore happy when this happened. This was also reflected in the comment used in the headline by the *Economic Times*.

Shoulder: **PM heaves a sigh of relief, NDA registers victory**
Main headline: **Soren complies with**
                         diktat, calls it quits

Another headline in the same genre was the one written for the suspension of a member of Parliament by the Biju Janata Dal President, Mr Naveen Patnaik (Fig. 3.9).

Comment can Reduce Clarity

The first casualty of comment is clarity. The headline writer uses turns of phrase that may sound meaningful and creative to those who are clued into news, but which may not be so well understood by the less accomplished readers.

When the Union Cabinet announced the government's decision in 2004 to introduce quotas for the economically backward classes, weeks before polls to five state assemblies, a Delhi newspaper wrote:

Ahead of polls, Govt approves quota for poor

At last Naveen acts, suspends Harihar

EXPRESS NEWS SERVICE

Bhubaneswar, Oct. 8: Chief Minister and Biju Janata Dal (BJD) president Naveen Patnaik suspended Lok Sabha member Harihar Swain from the party on Friday for indulging in anti-party activities.

Swain, who had switched over from the Congress to the BJD on the eve of the elections, embarras-

ncy. He had further alleged that the gap between the grass-roots workers and Patnaik is widening because he is not accessible.

Demand for disciplinary action against Swain was growing from the party leaders following his outbursts against Patnaik. Four ministers and six party MLAs had issued a joint statement on Thursday expressing shock over 'ind-

Fig. 3.9: *A commentative headline used by the* New Indian Express *regarding the action taken by the Biju Janata Dal President.*

There was nothing wrong with the clause 'ahead of polls', which implied that the government had taken the decision to influence voting. However, the headline writer did not use the term 'upper castes' in the headline. The headline therefore gave the impression that the quota was meant for the poor. In reality it was meant only for those poor who were not covered under the existing reservations–economically backward upper castes.

The *Hindu* captured the point better when it used the acronym EBCs for economically backward classes. However, the headline suffered because the acronym EBC is not popularly known.

Constitution to be amended to provide quota for EBCs

The *Indian Express* decided to comment upon the cabinet announcement. Its headline implied that the Cabinet announcement was akin to reserving the upper caste vote in the upcoming assembly elections. The pun was smart, but the meaning got diffused.

Reserved: Upper-caste vote

Comment should not be Offensive

When introducing comment in a headline, headline writers always run the danger of distorting meaning. An example of a bad headline was one that qualified bus operators as irresponsible because they went on a strike for the third time in a month.

Irresponsible bus operators strike work yet again

No newsman has the right to attribute motives in a headline. Insinuations must be taken out, even if they are made unwittingly.

SURPRISE HEADLINES

A headline writer must always seek to highlight the unusual. Hollywood weddings have been known for their glitz, glamour and often the bizarre. It was therefore not very surprising when ANI moved a news report quoting a website Eonline.com that Oscar winning actress Mira Sorvino had decided to marry an aspiring actor Christopher Backus. The interesting thing about Backus was that he was working as a waiter at a restaurant that the actress visited.

The headline writer did not focus on the fact that the marriage was between a star and an aspiring star, but between a celebrity and a waiter. The headline was like a storyline from a successful Hollywood romance.

Hollywood actress marries waiter

HINGLISH HEADLINES

A newspaper is the finest reflection of a country's culture, its habits, its speech, its attire and its lifestyle. It not only mirrors these trends on its news pages but also records them for posterity. A turning of newspaper pages of the years gone by is like turning the pages of history.

It is therefore not surprising to note that English newspapers today have started using more Hindi words not only in the body of the story but also in headlines. This trend can only be expected to grow in the coming years as the English spoken in India gets more and more Indianized. The Oxford English Dictionary has already started compiling a list of those Indian words that have become a part of the English language—and this list is growing with every passing year.

The headlines that use Hindi words are informally called Hinglish headlines, a term coined from the words Hindi and English. Since these headlines reflect the language that Indians are speaking today, they provide greater immediacy and freshness. For instance, when Mr Somnath Chatterjee became the Speaker of the Lok Sabha, members started addressing him as Somnathji, the Hindi term used as an address for elders. Earlier, his colleagues from Bengal used to address him as Somnath *da*, which is the Bengali address to show respect for elders. The *Telegraph* captured this change brilliantly in this headline:

Somnath, from da **to** ji

The popularity of these words flow from their pan-Indian recognition. In fact, their acceptance can be seen from the fact that even the *Hindu* uses them, though its readership is largely composed of South Indians whose mother tongue is not Hindi. For a feature on non-Indian daughters-in-law, the *Hindu* came up with this Hinglish headline (Fig. 3.10):

Phoren *bahu*, **desi** *saas*

Phoren *bahu*, desi *saas*

How do parents react to non-Indian daughters-in-law? Read on

"I GOT this vague e-mail from my son Vivek in Kuala Lumpur," Geetha Ragaraman says, looking glum. "It said, 'If you have a non-Indian daughter-in-law, how would you feel?' I didn't know what to make of it." The next mail, however, left no doubts. It said, "I like this British girl, she is wonderful. Her name is Catherine Corbett." Geetha's eyes light up at the mention of the name. Then came the photographs. "I liked her face a lot. You can say it was

'Far from seeing the cultural differences as a problem, I see this mix as a blessing'

— Catherine

that I wouldn't be free to make my own decisions with Indian in-laws! However, Amma has been marvellous. She offers advice and suggestions, but does not try to command us in any way."

Adjustment

"Adjustment is no big problem," says Edith, the chubby Hungarian Fulbright scholar preparing for the big day with Subbu. "I have known Subbu for 5 years. I have always been interested in religion — I took a course on India." She met Subbu at the Arizona college campus, switched from Psychology to Religious Studies, learned Sanskrit,

'Initially language was a problem, we are good friends now'

— Mrs. Subramaniam about Nahed

wedding went off well ... have lived happily ... years and two children.

The Egyptian bride ... born in Chennai. But four extended stays ... the U.S. helped. "Language was a problem ... Nahed knew little English ... we are good friends ... took me to her ... would cook rice, dal ... before going to ... would close my eyes to the fridge. We appreciate

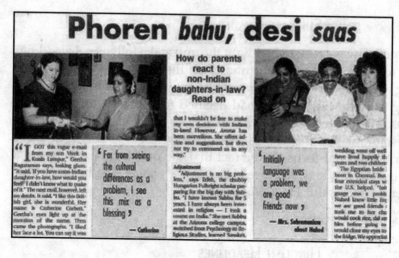

Fig. 3.10: *A Hinglish headline used in the* Hindu.

Newspapers are now using lyrics from popular Hindi films to write headlines. The *Indian Express* in its Sunday magazine used one such captivating lyric (Fig. 3.11) while the *Times of India*, with over 150 years of history behind it, now uses Hinglish headlines even on the edit page (Fig. 3.12). It surely is a sign of changing times.

Yeh hai Bombay Meri Jaan

Suketu Mehta's sprawling biography captures the essence of Bombay, finds **Coomi Kapoor**

comes the downside, an extortion threat from gangster Abu Salem, who even forbids two of his stars, Preity Zinta and Roshan, from going abroad to promote the film. Dutt finally uses his good offices to get Chopra removed from the mafia's hit list.

Mehta marvels at the irony of a world in which on the one hand Dutt appears regularly before the TADA courts since he is accused of conspiring against the state and on the other is invited by President Narayanan to Rashtrapati Bhavan and patted for making a patriotic film like Mission Kashmir.

The driving force of Bombay has always been dhanda — only the occupations keep

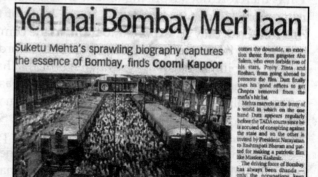

Fig. 3.11: *A headline based on a Hindi song used in the Sunday section of the* Indian Express.

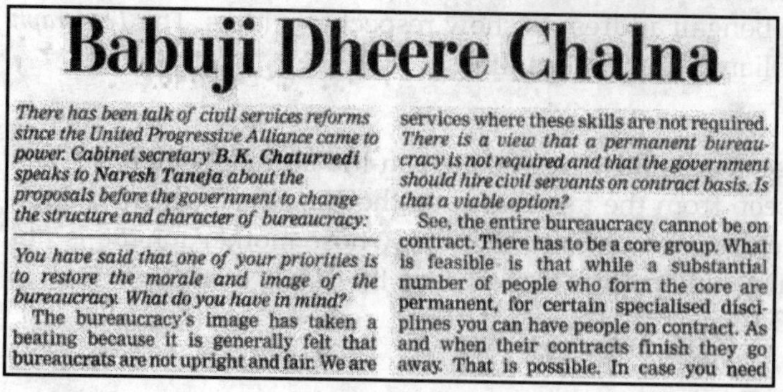

Babuji Dheere Chalna

There has been talk of civil services reforms since the United Progressive Alliance came to power. Cabinet secretary ***B.K. Chaturvedi*** *speaks to* ***Naresh Taneja*** *about the proposals before the government to change the structure and character of bureaucracy:*

You have said that one of your priorities is to restore the morale and image of the bureaucracy. What do you have in mind?

The bureaucracy's image has taken a beating because it is generally felt that bureaucrats are not upright and fair. We are services where these skills are not required.

There is a view that a permanent bureaucracy is not required and that the government should hire civil servants on contract basis. Is that a viable option?

See, the entire bureaucracy cannot be on contract. There has to be a core group. What is feasible is that while a substantial number of people who form the core are permanent, for certain specialised disciplines you can have people on contract. As and when their contracts finish they go away. That is possible. In case you need

Fig. 3.12: *A line from a Hindi film song used on the edit page of the* Times of India.

SIDEBARS

Sidebars are related stories run along with the main story. They are generally short and highlight a related point. Sidebars are usually placed in the belly of the main story so as to establish the connection with the main story.

The headline of the sidebar therefore has to be written in a slightly different manner. First, the sidebar is short; therefore the headline should be written in one or two decks in a small point size. Second, the headline need not mention the subject of the story since it is already stated in the headline of the main story.

For instance, the *Times of India* ran two reports on the one-day cricket series that was played between India and Pakistan in 2005. The main report stated that only two Pakistani fans had bought tickets for the Ahmedabad match. There was also a related report. It was about the last one-day match which was to be played at the Ferozeshah Kotla ground in Delhi and against which an appeal had been filed in the Supreme Court. It so happened that the Supreme Court dismissed the appeal on the same day. The newspaper therefore ran a sidebar with a simple headline:

SC clears Kotla

The headline did not need any context. That was provided by the main story (Fig. 3.13).

Only one Pak couple at today's one-day tie

By Peter Pears and Sourav Mukherjee/ TNN

Ahmedabad: Spotting a Pakistani fan among the 48,000 cheering spectators at the fourth Indo-Pak ODI in Motera on Tuesday will be the proverbial hunt for a needle in the haystack.

The Gujarat Cricket Association officials said the 500 tickets kept aside for Pak visitors have remained untouched. "A month ago, the BCCI messaged us for 300 tickets, but there's no communication since then," GCA secretary Vikram Patel said. "Right now, only a couple have approached us for tickets."

SC clears Kotla

New Delhi: Clearing the last-minute cloud over safety of spectators during the India-Pakistan ODI in Delhi on April 17, the Supreme Court on Monday refused to stall the match as the Centre and Municipal Corporation of Delhi said the Ferozeshah Kotla Stadium was "absolutely" safe.
● Gladiatorial battle, page 15
● Weather could be decisive, page 15
● Motera no problem, page 15

Fig. 3.13: *A sidebar placed within the main story in the* Times of India.

Headline Writing

Chapter Highlights

Characteristics of label headlines

1. The subject alone is mentioned.
2. The verb is missing.
3. They are used when the space is limited.
4. They are commonly used in supplements.

Advantages of Descriptive Headlines

1. Provide more information.
2. Bring out the key points well.
3. Capture the essence of the story.
4. Generate reader interest.
5. Remove ambiguity.
6. Add colour.

Disadvantages of descriptive headlines

1. Use more space.
2. Need to be spread across multiple columns.
3. May result in the headline being written in a small point size.

Running story headline

1. It must focus on the latest development.
2. It should use link words to establish connection.

Advantages of link words/phrase

1. Act as a connecting thread.
2. Allow the main headline to focus on the day's developments.
3. Work as a useful navigation tool.

Use of link words/phrase

1. Used in the shoulder.
2. Used in the strapline.
3. Used in the middle of a story.

How to write a multiple-point headline

1. Select the most important point.
2. Write the main headline on this point.
3. Select the second most important point.
4. Use a strapline to convey this point.
5. Use a link word in the strapline or in the middle of the report if it is a running story.

Pros and cons commentative headlines

1. Comment should not be offensive.
2. Comment should not be at the expense of facts.
3. Comment should not make meaning incomprehensible.
4. Comment should be used in analytical stories since it adds meaning to a headline.

Points to note

1. Comment can add spice to a headline.
2. A smart turn of phrase can provide vibrancy.

HEADLINE EXERCISES

Label Headlines

Exercise 1

Go through one week's newspapers and locate five label headlines. Rewrite each headline by using a verb.

Exercise 2

Locate any three headlines that you rate as the best in the day's newspaper. Rewrite these headlines as label headlines. Indicate what has been lost in the process.

Descriptive Headlines

Exercise 1

Go through a fortnight's newspapers to locate 10 headlines where the writer has used adjectives and adverbs to embellish the headline.

Exercise 2

Go through a month's newspapers and locate five headlines where the writer has unnecessarily used adjectives and adverbs. Give reasons why you think so.

Exercise 3

Write a descriptive headline for the five news reports that follow using the given headline parameters:
Point size: 28
Case: Upper-lower
Number of letters per column: 6
Column width: 3
Number of decks: 2

News Report 1

NEW DELHI (IANS): It was billed as India's biggest ever public art auction and the organisers claimed it raised around $2 million (Rs. 96 million) though the exact figure was not immediately available.

The highest price paid – Rs. 4.25 million – at the Friday evening auction was for a painting titled 'Crucifixion' by the late Goan artist F.N. Souza, followed by 'Rani', an M.F. Husain canvas that went for Rs. 4 million.

'Stormy Landscape', also by Souza, was sold for Rs. 3.75 million.

A total of 125 paintings, sculptures and rare books were placed for auction.

Hollywood star Richard Gere was the surprise package at the auction that plans to raise $2 million in a single evening.

Wearing his trademark rimless glasses and dressed in a blue cotton shirt, dark blue jeans and dark blue suede shoes, complete with a slightly frayed baseball cap and a red coloured bag with Buddhist icons on his shoulder, Gere seemed perfectly at ease as he soaked in the atmosphere.

'I am here in an unofficial capacity. That's why I can't say anything. I am here just with a friend,' said the self-effacing Gere, his left wrist in a plaster cast.

News Report 2

THIRUVANANTHAPURAM (IANS): A team of doctors successfully performed a surgery to remove a cataract from the eye of a 32-year-old Himalayan bear, the latest in a series of such procedures on animals at the zoo here.

The four ophthalmologists removed the cataract from the right eye of the female bear named Bello. The same team had successfully performed similar surgery this year on a lion-tailed macaque, a tigress and a lioness.

The team of doctors, three of them from the Regional Institute of Ophthalmology led by K. Mahadevan, completed Sunday's surgery in just under 30 minutes.

"Though we had made arrangements for a special intra-ocular lens from a Vadodara-based manufacturer, we decided not to insert the lens. The bear is still under sedation and has been shifted to a new cage in the zoo hospital. She is fine," said Saju Kurian George, one of the doctors.

The two bears in Thiruvananthapuram Zoo were nearly blind due to cataract and corneal opacity. With the operation, one of them can now see.

The zoo authorities now plan to have the other bear undergo the same operation.

All three animals that had undergone the cataract surgery are fine and can see properly.

Postoperative care is the most difficult part of these surgeries because it is easy for the animals to get infected. They are thus kept in a cage where it is difficult for them to move for a few days after the operation.

News Report 3

BANGALORE (ENS): It was almost as if the waters have washed away what politicians were using to hide in Bangalore. Set to host delegates from 18 countries for the showcase IT event 'Bangalore IT.in' opening on Wednesday, India's infotech capital floundered in rain water.

For a city whose crumbling infrastructure regularly threatens to fall off the state government radar, the three-day spell of showers couldn't have come at a worse time: just days after a bruising battle between Congress's big brother H D Deve Gowda — the chief guest on Wednesday — and Infosys chairman N R Narayana Murthy.

Even Gowda's attendance is in doubt. JD (S) convener Y S V Datta said Gowda would visit rain-affected areas from 8 am to 1 pm. "In his schedule, if he fails to attend the function, a written speech copy would be sent through Industries and Finance Minister P G R Sindhia," he said.

Palace Grounds, the venue for the IT.in event, located at a higher altitude than Hosur Road and considered safe ground, was itself a virtual swimming pool today. Even the approach road to Palace Grounds, the Airport Road, was a nightmare with its unfinished flyover and multiple traffic diversions.

The rain began late on Saturday night when the city received 12 cm of rainfall — well below its single-day record of 18. Two deaths, flooded roads and buildings, gridlocked traffic, disrupted power and telephone networks and there was chaos today, all after a mere 7.7 cm of rainfall, a teardrop in comparison to Mumbai's 94 cm in July this year.

Yet it still submerged Hosur Road, a part of NH7 and Bangalore's link to the Electronics City, where the campuses of its IT pride — Infosys, Wipro and other companies — are located.

Water from a breached lake bund beside the road engulfed a section of the highway. Bang in the middle is a chest-high water body. Two people drowned in the rushing waters here, the Bangalore police said.

By 6 pm on Tuesday, employees returning home from Electronics City were stuck in a 5-km traffic jam along the road — what normally is a 45-minute ride home became a four-hour ordeal.

Bangalore, of course, is only paying for its sins. Whenever it rains more than 5 cm, the years of unplanned development show up, particularly its lake beds indiscriminately converted into real estate.

News Report 4

HYDERABAD/SRISAILAM (ENS): After enjoying a week-long hospitality extended by the State Government for taking part in the historic peace talks, leaders of the CPI (Maoist) and Janashakti combine returned to their hideouts in the Nallamala forests on Wednesday.

The bonhomie and camaraderie between the police and the 'state guests' was noticeable at the Manjeera Guest House in Hyderabad as members of the People's Liberation Guerilla Army (PLGA) shook hands with the police before departure. Members of the Jana Natya Mandali, the cultural wing of the CPI (Maoist) party, sang for about half an hour before the convoy left the city.

The cordiality between Naxalites and police continued throughout the 250-km journey which began at 1 p.m. from the capital. There were as many as 20 vehicles in the convoy with a battery of mediapersons and about 15 policemen accompanying the extremists.

At 6 p.m, about 5 km before reaching Srisailam temple, located amidst thick forests in Kurnool district, policemen were asked to go back. The revolutionaries shook hands with the policemen and posed for photographs. The Naxalites then travelled 10 km further and stopped at China Arutla village.

Leaving the vehicles behind, they started walking on a kutcha road and after half a km, a young lad clad in lungi, holding aloft the party flag received them. Behind the boy was an armed dalam led by a senior functionary Ravi.

Even as the dalam members raised slogans 'Long Live armed struggle, Naxalbari ek hi rasta, Let us die for people, Long Live People's War,' Ravi and others handed over weapons including AK-47s to CPI-Maoist state secretary Ramakrishna and others and hugged them.

Several journalists who followed the Naxalite leaders from Hyderabad saw a row of armed Naxalites in olive green uniforms disturbing the quietness of a chilly night. At this point, mediamen were also asked to turn back. The Naxal leaders said that they would be trekking 10 to 12 km deep inside the forests throughout the night before reaching their area.

News Report 5

HYDERABAD (ENS): Broken glass pieces and furniture strewn all around, frightened in-patients and their anxious relatives, agitated employees discussing the future course of action, and a strong posse of police keeping a tab on visitors…

It was a tense situation at the Gandhi Hospital after the students of a private engineering college clashed with the hospital authorities following the death of a student. Perhaps for the first time in its 150 years of existence, the main entrance of the hospital was shut down.

The attack, which lasted for over half an hour, appeared to be planned as the miscreants went on a rampage with a few private television channels accompanying them.

By the time the doctors and hospital staff realised the gravity of the situation and organised themselves to stop the mayhem, the damage was already done.

The media personnel who went to cover the incident had to face the brunt of the medicos. "How can you give wrong information that the youth died due to our negligence without knowing the facts?" they countered.

As the patients' relatives came out for lunch on the hospital corridors, the students started breaking glass panes forcing them to run for cover.

But for patients like Suhasini, who lost her girl child two days ago, there was no escape. "The glass pieces fell all over my body," said Suhasini who is in a state of shock.

The attackers did not stop there. They wrenched the name plates and damaged the door of a room in the blood bank. Even the wooden partition separating the generators in the ladies toilet was torn off. "We never expected this. It is a black day for the hospital," said a dazed bio statistician Neela Veni.

Arogyam, one of the attenders, says: "The entire incident resembled a film. I don't understand how they could do this to a hospital. Now it will take at least a week for everything to return to normalcy," he said.

Running Stories

Exercise 1

Go through one month's newspapers and locate three running stories that have made headlines for three days or more. For each story indicate the style used by the newspaper to provide continuity. This can be use of navigation heads, shoulders or straplines. Also, examine the appropriateness of the headlines in highlighting the latest developments.

Exercise 2

Write a shoulder-based headline for each of the following three running stories using the parameters given below. The headline for the first story need not include any link word and can be without the shoulder.

Main headline
Point size: 28
Case: Upper-lower
Number of letters per column: 6
Column width: 2
Number of decks: 2
Shoulder
Point size: 14
Case: Upper-lower
Number of letters per column: 14
Column width: 2
Number of decks: 1

News Report/Day 1

GHAZIABAD, Oct 23 (PTI): Thirty-two children have died of a mysterious disease over the last two days while several others have been admitted to various hospitals in parts of western Uttar Pradesh, official sources said.

As many as 14 children have died in Khekra town in Baghpat district, eight in Muzaffarnagar and 10 in Saharanpur due to a disease which has symptoms similar to that of encephalitis, meningitis and cholera, they said.

Over 100 children with complaints of severe headache, fever and vomitting were brought to health care centres and government hospitals in Meerut, Baghpat, Muzaffarnagar and Garhmukteshwar districts, the sources said.

Six ailing children were admitted to the Meerut Government Hospital, Baghpat District Magistrate Kamini Ratan told PTI. Three children from Garhmukteshwar have also been admitted here.

The disease is a result of inflammation of the brain membranes and patients generally vomit blood, S K Arora, Director, Health, Meerut division told PTI.

The disease is prevalent among those residing in unhygienic conditions, he said.

News Report/Day 2

GHAZIABAD, Oct 24 (PTI): Sixteen more children succumbed to a mysterious disease in several districts of western Uttar Pradesh raising the toll to 48 during the last three days, official sources said.

Two more children died in a hospital last night in Saharanpur where the toll has crossed 20, one each succumbed in Noida and Ghaziabad to the disease which has symptoms similar to that of Meningitis and Cholera, they said.

Twelve children have died in Bulandshahr, District Magistrate Abhishek Singh said.

District Magistrate, Baghpat, Kamini Ratan Chauhan told PTI that the number of ailing children was still rising although no new deaths have been reported in the district.

Over 100 children with complaints of severe headache, fever and vomitting have already been brought to health care centres and government hospitals in Meerut, Muzaffarnagar and Garhmukteshwar districts, the sources said.

News Report/Day 3

NEW DELHI, Oct 25 (ENS): The Union Health Ministry has sent a five-member team to Baghpat in Uttar Pradesh following reports of the death of 13 children due to a 'mysterious fever'.

The team comprises three members from the National Institute of Communicable Diseases, including a microbiologist and an epidemiologist, and two paediatricians from Delhi. According to officials in the Health Ministry, the team was sent to investigate the cause of the deaths following a request from the chief medical officer and district commissioner of the area.

Another team from the National Institute of Virology is likely to visit the area in the next two-three days.

81

al encephalitis is said to be behind the death of the children,
all below the age of five years.

"The disease history is very short. The children had high grade fever and vomitting.
They later went into coma and died within six to 12 hours," said an official.

"As virological analysis takes time, doctors in the area have been asked to treat the
patients symptomatically," the official added.

According to officials, while sporadic incidents had been reported since October 13, the
death of three children on October 18 raised the alarm. According to Health Ministry
officials, the disease has not spread to other places as reported in a section of the media.
Three cases have been reported from GTB Hospital in Delhi, but "they were from Baghpat",
they said.

Exercise 2

Write a strapline-based headline for each of the following four running stories using
the parameters given below. The headline for the first story need not include any
link word and can be without the strapline.

Main headline
Point size: 30
Case: Upper-lower
Number of letters per column: 5
Column width: 5
Number of decks: 1

Shoulder
Point size: 14
Case: Upper-lower
Number of letters per column: 14
Column width: 5
Number of decks: 1

News Report/Day 1

NEW DELHI, Oct 20 (PTI): About 35 more rocket shells were found in metal scrap in three
trucks that arrived at Bhushan Steel Factory in Ghaziabad, where a bomb exploded killing
10 people on September 30.

However, none of the 35 shells discovered in the three trucks that arrived at the factory
yesterday were found to be live, Ghaziabad SP Umesh Shrivastava told PTI.

"The shells have been handed over to the Army who have taken them to a secluded
spot on the banks of Yamuna river near Loni where they will be destroyed," the SP said.

These shells will be destroyed along with nearly 100 shells recovered over the past few
weeks in the district.

The recovery of 35 more shells follows an explosion at the factory yesterday and
recovery of six more live munitions by the Army and the police.

News report/Day 2

LUCKNOW, Oct 21 (PTI): Three persons were injured in a blast in a steel factory in Hamirpur district of Uttar Pradesh today, a senior police officer said.

The blast took place in Rimjhim steel factory, about 15 kms from here this afternoon, Superintendent of Police, Hamirpur, Arun Kumar told PTI on phone.

Five truck loads of scrap material had arrived at the factory from Meerut a couple of days ago and the possibility of explosives being present in the scrap material could not be ruled out, he said, adding investigations were on.

Neither the factory owner nor the labourers informed the police about the blast. The police reached the scene only after getting information from other sources, he said.

News Report/Day 3

BHAVNAGAR (Gujarat), Oct 22 (PTI): In the biggest recovery in Gujarat, 48 shells were recovered from two different factory-cum-scrap yard premises in Bhavnagar district today including 36 from the factory where a blast had killed two labourers and injured three on Wednesday, police has said.

"Thirty-six shells were recovered from India Power Ltd factory in Navagaam area, where the blast had occurred, and 12 were from Rishi rolling-mill in Sihor town nearby," Bhavnagar district Superintendent of police Hasmukh Patel told PTI.

Bomb disposal teams have been dispatched to both the sites, the SP said. He said in both the recoveries, some of the shells were found half empty. The SP said that 36 shells were found from different parts of the factory.

He, however, could not ascertain the origin of the shells and said that this was subject to investigation.

News Report/Day 4

RAIPUR (Chhattisgarh), Oct 24 (PTI): A total of 42 shells, including 28 live, were recovered from a pond on the outskirts of the city, police said today.

"Police fished out 42 shells from a pond located on the national highway near Bemta village under Simga police station area yesterday," Raipur District Superintendent of Police Ashok Juneja told PTI here.

With this the total number of explosives recovered from the district have gone up to 114, he said.

All the shells were kept in three jute bags and one plastic bag, police said adding, the explosives must have been thrown into the pond by anyone involved in the scrap trading.

The villagers of Bemta noticed the bags after the water in the pond started receding and informed the Simga police who subsequently fished out the bags, Juneja said.

Experts from National Security Guard and Jabalpur Ordnance Factory have arrived here to destroy the recovered explosive materials, he said.

Chhattisgarh Government had on October 13 handed over the case of explosives recovery to the CBI.

Headlines for Multiple-point Leads

Exercise 1

Go through a fortnight's newspapers to locate five news reports that have a multiple-point lead. Analyse each headline to understand how the headline writer chose the news point(s) to write the headline.

Exercise 2

Write two headlines for each of the following three news reports using the following headline parameters:

Headline 1
Point size: 28
Case: Upper-lower
Number of letters per column: 6
Column width: 5
Number of decks: 1

Headline 2
Main headline
Point size: 30
Case: Upper-lower
Number of letters per column: 5
Column width: 4
Number of decks: 1

Strapline
Point size: 14
Case: Upper-lower
Number of letters per column: 14
Column width: 4
Number of decks: 1

News Report 1

NEW DELHI: In a bid to put the NDA and its Convenor George Fernandes on the defensive, the Centre today decided to scrap the commission inquiring into the Tehelka expose on defence deals and asked the CBI to probe into the tapes revealing the role of "various personalities".

"The Cabinet Committee on Political Affairs (CCPA) has decided not to extend the term of the commission headed by Justice S N Phukan, which expired on October 3," Law Minister H R Bharadwaj told reporters alleging that the NDA government had "misdirected" the inquiry as it wanted to "delay" and "shield" the then defence minister.

The commission's term expired yesterday and the government has decided not to extend its tenure any further.

"The matter will now be probed in detail by CBI in an independent manner and the government will provide it the tapes used in the sting operation conducted by the web portal Tehelka," he said. After getting the tapes from the commission, which would wind up very soon, the government would forward them to the investigating agency, he said adding it was for the CBI to decide the course of inquiry including registration of FIR.

"We would like the agency to speedily complete the probe," he said but gave no time frame for it.

News Report 2

GUWAHATI (UNI): In unabated terrorist violence in Assam for the third consecutive day, six more people were gunned down and nine injured last night even as the Centre decided to go the whole hog against insurgents by formulating a long-term multi-pronged strategy and coordinating efforts with all northeastern states.

Suspected ultras of the National Democratic Front of Bodoland (NDFB) and the United Liberation Front of Asom (ULFA) gunned down six people at Gelapukhuri in Sonitpur district of Upper Assam around midnight last night taking the death toll to 70 in the state in the last three days of terrorist violence.

Union Home Minister Shivraj Patil, who toured Assam and Nagaland yesterday and today to assess the situation after Saturday's bomb explosions and firing incidents in which 60 people were killed and more than 100 injured, arrived here again today from Dimapur to take stock of the situation.

The Home Minister visited Dhubri and other areas in Lower Assam, which have been rocked by militant violence during the last two days, and reviewed the situation along with Assam Chief Minister Tarun Gogoi and senior civil and security officials.

Assuring the state government of all possible help to contain the violence, the Home Minister said the door for talks "without any condition" with insurgent outfits like ULFA was "still open." He said a long-term multi-pronged strategy was being worked out to check terrorism.

"The government of India will do everything to help the Assam government… If anybody comes with any condition and wants to hold talks, we will not accept. The talks should be held without any condition," he said.

Asked whether the government was still willing to hold talks with the ULFA, Mr Patil said the Centre had not "closed the doors for talks...It is our duty to save human lives and innocent people."

News Report 3

NEW DELHI (ENS): The Urban Development Ministry has proposed the reopening of four India Presses in various parts of the country, which had been closed down by the previous NDA government after they ran up huge losses.

Two of the India Presses that the UPA Government is considering reopening are the Government of India Forms Store and Office of the Assistant Director (Outside Printing) in Kolkata. The other two are the Government of India Presses in Shimla and Gangtok.

The NDA government had decided to shut down the government-run presses in September 2002. While four of them were ultimately shut, five of them were merged.

Three other Textbook Presses under the Urban Development Ministry in Chandigarh, Bhubaneswar and Mysore were transferred to the state governments with the clause that if they did not accept them by 2003, they too would be shut.

The Cabinet note on reopening the presses has been circulated among the ministries concerned, including the Finance Ministry, for comments. Sources said there have been several representations from the state governments to revive the printing presses.

Exercise 3

Write a headline that highlights the cause and effect in the given news report. The headline should be written using the following parameters:

Main headline
Point size: 30
Case: Upper-lower
Number of letters per column: 5
Column width: 5
Number of decks: 1

NEW DELHI (UNI): Chief Election Commissioner T S Krishna Murthy will "witness" the United States' Presidential elections on November two following Prime Minister Manmohan Singh's intervention to clear his visit, overruling objections by the External Affairs Ministry.

The CEC had approached Dr Singh after the External Affairs Ministry had refused to clear his visit, stating that accepting the US invitation would place no obligation on India to reciprocate the American gesture at a later stage.

A PMO official confirmed Dr Singh's intervention to clear the visit of the CEC who is likely to leave on October 28.

Commission sources said there was no substance in the objections by the foreign office as this was not the first time the CEC would be in the United States at the invitation of Washington to witness the Presidential poll.

Mr Krishna Murthy's immediate predecessors, Mr J M Lyngdoh and Mr M S Gill, had witnessed the American Presidential elections, they pointed out.

Commentative Stories

Exercise 1

Go through a fortnight's newspapers and locate three headlines where a comment has been used. Rewrite the headlines without using the comment.

Exercise 2

Locate any three news reports where the writer has analysed important political developments. Write a commentative headline for each report in the same point size and column width as used in the newspaper.

Exercise 3

Write a commentative headline for each of the following three reports using the given parameters:
Point size: 30
Case: Upper-lower
Number of letters per column: 5
Column width: 3
Number of decks: 2

News Report 1

NEW DELHI (UNI): Pointing out that the existing state laws on abolition of Devdasi system in Maharashtra, Andhra Pradesh and Karnataka are woefully inadequate and suffer from loopholes, an NHRC Report has suggested a comprehensive Central legislation to abolish the system of 'divine prostitution', perpetuated by temple priests.

"Such a law may also bring within its ambit other customary practices leading to sexual exploitation of Scheduled Castes and Scheduled Tribes women," says the Report on Prevention of Atrocities Against Scheduled Castes, prepared by a former bureaucrat K B Sharma for the NHRC.

But until a Central law is in position, the NHRC may direct the state governments concerned to amend their existing laws, remove loopholes, make it more stringent and activate the enforcement machinery to implement it effectively, Mr Sharma, associated with the uplift of Dalits in Bihar, has suggested.

He says the states should also, through the coordinated efforts of their departments of Scheduled Castes Welfare, Woman and Child Development, and Rural Development, launch a massive awareness programme, particularly directed at the vulnerable communities, for abolition of 'divine prostitution' system and availability of schemes for the rehabilitation of the liberated Devdasis.

The programme should provide information on the individuals and organisations, the women affected by the system, potential victims and their guardians should approach for seeking intervention of the government, he says.

"The temple priests should be targeted in this campaign for conveying the message that they incur criminal liability in encouraging or conniving at this practice," he says, and calls for roping in NGOs and social activists in the awareness campaign.

News Report 2

NEW DELHI (UNI): The National Commission for Women has expressed shock at inhuman bonded labour still prevailing in Tamil Nadu and recommended the identification, release and rehabilitation of bonded labourers in the state within three months.

"It is shocking that three decades after the passing of the Bonded Labour Abolition Act the inhuman practice is still persisting in its most primitive and vicious form in a progressive state like Tamil Nadu," the Commission observed in its report about public hearing regarding the prevalence of bonded labourers in the rice mills of Thiruvelur.

It directed immediate release of all the labourers who appeared before it and those whose families have already filed complaints to RDO and their rehabilitation within a fortnight.

The Commission called for identification and release of other bonded labourers in the rice mills of red hills within two weeks and their rehabilitation within two months.

"Identification and release of all bonded labourers in rice mills throughout the state within two months. Rehabilitation of all the bonded labourers within the state in three months," were the other recommendations made by the Commission.

It called for prosecuting the employers under the provisions of Bonded Labour Act, SC/ST Prevention of Atrocities Act, Factories Act. The NCW said that all the arrears due and payable by the owners of rice mills under the Minimum Wages Act alongwith the penalty as prescribed under the Act be secured.

The Commission has recommended strict action against the district officials who have failed to implement the Bonded Labour Act.

News Report 3

NEW DELHI (IANS): The National Human Rights Commission (NHRC) has accused the police of discriminating against people from the socially underprivileged classes, bordering on sabotaging justice.

An NHRC report on prevention of atrocities against the Scheduled Castes (Dalits) has found that the police went out of their way to protect members of high caste Hindus who perpetrate violence against Dalits seeking justice.

"The problem starts with registration of the case itself. Police resort to various machinations to discourage Scheduled Castes and Scheduled Tribes from registering a case, to dilute the seriousness of the violence and shield the real accused (who may be caste Hindus)," it said.

If at all the police register a case, they refuse to file cases under the Scheduled Castes and Scheduled Tribes (Prevention of Atrocities) Act, 1989, so as to avoid punitive measures against the accused, the report claimed.

They only register the cases under the Protection of Civil Rights Act, a much leaner act.

The failure results in the perpetrators being punished with a lesser sentence, rejection of claims for compensation by the victims, and release of the accused on bail.

But the most obvious form of state violence against Dalits was the treatment meted out to them in police custody in connection with criminal case, petty cases of theft and minor offences, the report said.

It claimed that police reserved barbaric interrogation methods for their Dalit subjects, inflicting serious injuries on them that often end in their deaths.

"The custodial deaths are covered up usually," it said, adding that killing of Dalits in gun battles was the next best favourite means of elimination used by the police.

Police also act with vengeance against Dalit activists fighting for their rights, by invoking harsh provisions of the law including the National Security Act, it said.

The NHRC study said the apathy and bias was not confined to police personnel alone, but extends to other agencies of the government, including the district civil administration.

4
KINDS OF HEADLINES – II

QUOTES AS HEADLINES

Quotes are used sparsely in headlines. This is because they are used to embellish a news point and are not the story by themselves. It is therefore important to select a quote carefully. A quote when used in a headline should evoke strong emotions such as horror, anger, joy, hate—emotions that get diluted when a quote is paraphrased. The following points need to be kept in mind when a quote is used to write a headline.

Stories Built on Quotes

It is very rare when an entire news report is built around a single quote. However, when that happens it is important that the quote should be used as the headline. A case in point is the report about the Director General of Police (DGP) in Madhya Pradesh who played on the word 'minor' in a rape case involving his subordinate. The DGP was quoted as saying that the 13-year-old girl who was allegedly raped by a police officer and his friends was 'a minor but not that minor'.

The DGP's words expectedly caused outrage. The agency moved the report with the following headline:

Madhya Pradesh police's new definition for minor in rape case

The headline clearly lacked spirit. It read more like legalese than the headline of a story that had stirred a great debate in the state. The Newindpress.com headline writer went for the jugular by placing the DGP's words in his mouth.

DIG rapes 13-year-old, DGP says she was 'a minor but not that minor'

It was not surprising that the story was the most highly read story on the website that day.

Statement Made by Unknown Persons

A small proportion of news reports in a newspaper revolve around common people.

These people are not celebrities, who occupy miles of newspaper space every day, but common men and women who shoot into the limelight on account of crimes committed by them, or when they happen to be victims of unexpected calamities like accidents, floods, fires or earthquakes.

Reporters drag them on to newspaper pages to bring out the human face of the tragedy. In such cases, the quotes should be selected for their emotional content— content that brings out the dark, the bad or the ugly side of the incident, not to forget the good side when there is one. These quotes can be run as stand alone quotes, because no one will be able to identify these people by their names.

A good example was the quote that was used to convey a rapist's fear of being hanged. This rapist, who had kidnapped a 12-year-old girl, lost his nerve when he watched a news bulletin on television that said the Supreme Court had sentenced a Kolkata man accused of rape and murder to death by hanging. He surrendered to the police. The headline as moved by the news agency was straight. A direct quote would have injected drama and outrage.

Original
Fearing hanging, rapist returns with victim
Revised
'I only raped her a few times, I don't want to hang'

If, however, attribution is to be used then it should be based on the victim's functional identity as arrived at in the story. Thus, a statement made by a girl who has been raped should be attributed as one made by the rape victim; while the comment made by a man who has been pulled out of a house razed by an earthquake should be attributed to a quake survivor.

Use of Attribution

It is important to identify the person who has made a statement. It sparks reader interest and adds value to a headline. Very often headline writers defend their work by saying that the details are available in the story. This is an unprofessional approach and must be discouraged in all newsrooms. Each headline must be complete in itself. Here are two headlines where the subject's name is missing. What is the reader to surmise from them?

'I want to be a part of this team in whatever way'
'I will direct a film when I have enough money'

Incidentally, two of India's most recognized faces made these statements. But for their fans to zero in on the story, the headlines needed attribution. The attribution was also needed for other readers.

Revised headline with attribution
I want to be a part of this team in whatever way: Ganguly
I will direct a film when I have enough money: Shahrukh

Attribution can be avoided when the headline is placed over a large photograph of the celebrity. The photograph then works as a headline prop enabling the reader to deduce who the speaker is. This is a format that is generally followed by magazines or feature sections of newspapers. However, this format is also being used for hard news stories now. The *Hindu* used a large photograph of Dr Manmohan Singh when he addressed his first press conference after becoming the prime minister and ran a quote above it as the headline without attributing it to the prime minister (Fig. 4.1).

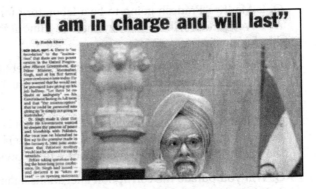

Fig. 4.1: *A direct quote of the Prime Minister, Dr Manmohan Singh, used by the* Hindu *as the lead headline.*

But this is not a good practice. A news headline must be complete in itself. A reader must know who has made the statement at first glance. Headlines that fail to do so are bad headlines. Also, the single quotes should be dropped when the speaker's name is used in the headline.

Attribution is also essential for quotations taken from remarks made by committees, panels, organizations, officials, etc. It is important that such comments are properly anchored so that the reader knows the source. An example of a quote that left readers nonplussed was about a remark made by a panel of scholars appointed by the Human Resources Development Minister, Mr Arjun Singh, to review the changes made in history books by the earlier NDA government. The panel found that only nine of the 89 pages in the National Council of Educational Research and Training (NCERT) book spoke about south India whereas the remaining 80 pages were devoted to the history of north India. The headline writer correctly zeroed in on the news point in this report. However, the headline writer made a mistake by leaving out the attribution in the headline. The result was that the headline seemed like a statement being made by a politician at a public meeting or during the course of an interview.

Original
'History of India can't be history of North India'
Preferred
South India ignored in history book, finds review panel

Stories in Question-answer Format

Direct speech has a freshness that is lost whenever it is paraphrased. That is why headline writers must choose a statement that best expresses the subject's view on a controversial issue and use it as a quote.

The *Week* carried the following interview of the Bharatiya Janata Party (BJP) leader, Ms Uma Bharati, in its issue dated 14 December 2003.

Q. Is Madhya Pradesh going to be a laboratory for the BJP?
A. Development will be the key mantra. Hindutva is not something out of tune with development.

Q. How will you manage to tackle the huge debt left behind by the Digvijay regime?
A. That will be a real challenge but within a year I will bring the state's economy back on track.

Q. How different will chief minister Uma Bharati be from the Uma Bharati of Ayodhya?
A. I am still the Uma Bharati of Ayodhya. There is no change in me. The fervour I had shown during the Ayodhya movement will be present when I work to uplift the poor.

Q. Will you pursue the corruption allegations against Digvijay?
A. I am not going to be a vengeful chief minister. The law will decide on each and every case.

Ms Uma Bharati is not known to mince words. Even this brief interview that spanned a mere four questions were a headline writer's delight. It had two statements that were instant attention grabbers. These were:

'I am still the Uma Bharati of Ayodhya'
'I am not going to be a vengeful chief minister'

The *Week* rightly chose the first statement as the headline for the interview. In eight words it summed up the personality of the firebrand BJP leader. The sting would have been lost if the statement had been paraphrased as:

Sanyasin says she is still the Uma Bharati of Ayodhya
or
Uma Bharati says she has not changed from her Ayodhya days

The paraphrased headlines use more words to say the same thing, albeit in a slightly diluted manner. That is why the first choice for a report written in the question-answer format should be a headline that uses quotes.

Editing of Quotes

A question that is commonly asked is: can two different remarks made by a subject during the course of an interview be run as a single headline? The answer is yes. There is no harm in using two related statements on an issue as long as the meaning conveyed is the same as that intended by the subject. Also, the two remarks must be separated by an ellipsis so that the reader realizes that the two were not made in a sequence.

Indian cricket captain Sourav Ganguly was the toast of the country after the team's brilliant performance in Australia during the 2003–04 series. In an interview to the *Week* he was asked to explain the reason for the team's winning streak. Ganguly's answer to the question is reproduced below:

> **Q.** When you started out as captain, we were not winning that many matches. Now, it is becoming a habit.
>
> **A.** When we started out, we were winning in India, we were winning One-Day competitions – remember we beat Australia in 2001 when I took over – but obviously we have become a completely different side now. With time, everybody has grown. I think all of us are playing our best cricket at this stage. That is why the team is winning.

The headline writer picked two sentences to convey the thrust of Ganguly's answer. Since the points were taken from two different sentences an ellipsis was used to join the points.

We have become a completely different side now...everybody has grown: Ganguly

There may be times when two sentences run together can be juxtaposed to convey the meaning without an ellipsis. This is what was done with the actress Aishwarya Rai's answer to a question posed by IANS:

> "I put on some weight in hospital. Gurinder Chadha wanted that filled up, prosperous look for *Bride & Prejudice*. Then Rituparno Ghosh also wanted the same look for *Raincoat*. In that film I look like a well-fed Bihari housewife."

Headline after editing the quote

In *Raincoat*, I look like a well-fed Bihari housewife: Aishwarya

Another question that is often asked is: can a remark made by a subject be edited so as to accommodate the quote in the space available? The answer once again is yes. The statement can be shortened to bring out the most newsworthy point.

Actress Preity Zinta in an interview to IANS explained why she worked extra hard when she went on the stage. The sentence chosen for the headline was weak. But the headline writer edited it well.

Q: You prepare a lot before going on stage?

A: That's because I know I'm not too great on stage. The others, Shah Rukh and Saif, are brilliant on stage. Rani, too, is a very good dancer. Arjun and Priyanka have a great presence. Throw me in, and we've quite a group.

Sentence chosen: **That's because I know I'm not too great on stage**

Edited headline: **I'm not too great on stage: Preity Zinta**

But there is a limit on the kind of change that can be made. The most that can be removed from the quote are articles or auxiliary verbs. The headline writer can also consider removing adjectives or adverbs if their removal does not dilute the comment made by a subject. A headline writer should never change the meaning, literal or implied, when editing a quote for reasons of space, for sharpening it, or while joining two statements to communicate related points.

Use of Partial Quotes

Headline writers use partial quotes for two reasons: to stress important points made by a speaker; and two, to retain the flavour of the comment. For instance, there were reports in some newspapers in 2004 that Bahujan Samaj Party (BSP) leader, Ms Mayawati, had chosen a 'successor' to continue the party work in case she was arrested. The reports, of course, were not clear as to what the successor's precise role would be. Therefore, when Ms Mayawati refuted the reports as baseless, the headline writer correctly used the word successor in partial quotes.

Mayawati denies report on 'successor'

Another headline where a partial quote correctly captured the news point was on the meeting of the US Secretary of State, Mr Colin Powell, with the External Affairs Minister, Mr Natwar Singh (Fig. 4.2). The *New Indian Express* report, which combined analysis with news development, stated the following in the third paragraph:

> Meanwhile, highly placed sources here said India was ready and willing to transform the Line of Control into a 'softer kind of line' which 'bridges, instead of divides' the people of Kashmir who live on either side.

Headline used: **India ready for 'softer' LoC**

Fig. 4.2: *A partial quote used as part of the headline in the* New Indian Express.

QUESTION HEADLINES

Question headlines are not favoured in several newsrooms. The common refrain is that they leave a reader guessing. This is not what newspapers want. They would like the reader to grasp the meaning of each headline clearly. But this does not mean that question headlines should not be used. They have several virtues that cannot be overlooked. Of course, to be effective they must be used sparingly. Some of the attributes of question headlines are discussed below.

Evoke Curiosity

A question headline is a great way to evoke curiosity. It hints at motives, conspiracies, deals that are being secretly negotiated, behind-the-scenes shenanigans, etc. At the same time, a question headline keeps the newspaper free from the possibility of defamation because the newspaper is not supplying answers or making a statement of fact; it is only asking questions, even if the questions happen to be loaded.

That is why question headlines are highly effective in mystery stories that capture reader interest. For instance, a newspaper will hesitate to state bluntly that a public figure involved in a hit-and-run case was drunk unless the police have provided this information based on an alcohol analysis test. It will be easier for the newspaper to raise the issue as an interesting question.

Did the minister visit a bar before the accident?

A headline like this keeps a running story alive. However, such headlines should be used sparingly. They show that the newspaper has something to hide, has incomplete information or has based its story on speculation that is reasonably sound but not enough to be considered a fact.

Suited for Speculative Stories

There was much speculation in the media of infighting in the BJP's second rung leadership in the second half of 2004. Rival camps were working overtime feeding reports that the then BJP President, Mr Venkaiah Naidu, was feeling insecure at the response generated by Ms Uma Bharati's Tiranga Yatra. There was also speculation that the BJP had launched the Savarkar Yatra under the leadership of Ms Sushma Swaraj to steal part of the Tiranga Yatra thunder.

All this was in the realm of speculation. No leader was willing to go on record and acknowledge that the story was either correct or incorrect. But there were enough political straws to make a juicy story. The reporter had the luxury to hedge behind statements like 'it is reported', 'it is understood', etc. The headline writer had no such subterfuges. That is why the headline writer chose the question headline to make the point.

Is Venkaiah Naidu on his way out?

Computer Express similarly used a question headline on the sale of inkjet printers (Fig. 4.3). The story pointed out the rise in sales of Canon inkjet printers in smaller cities and asked the question:

Can Canon shake HP's hold on inkjets?

The publication had made a speculative point without committing itself.

Fig. 4.3: *A question headline used by* Computer Express *on the sale of inkjet printers.*

To Provoke

Question headlines are not always written when a newspaper wants to hedge facts. They are sometimes also used to provoke and make a reader think. A great headline in this category was the one that was written for Greg Chappell's column in *Outlook* (Fig. 4.4). The column assessed the fortunes of different teams participating in the ICC Champions Trophy 2004.

Chappell, like a true-blooded Australian, took it for granted that Australia would lift the trophy. To him the battle was not for the number one slot; rather, the battle was to identify the team that would challenge the Australian supremacy. The *Outlook* headline writer rose to the occasion and captured this provocative point well in the headline:

Who will be no 2?

Useful for Pro-and-con Reports

Question headlines can also be used for analytical stories where a writer brings out the pluses and minuses of an issue but does not provide a conclusion. In such cases the headline writer has no option but to raise a question, and let the reader decide after going through the story.

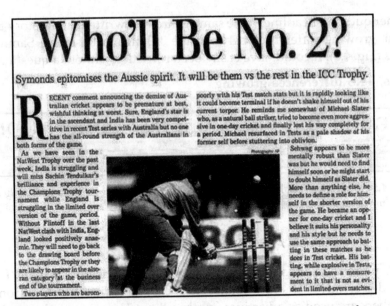

Who'll Be No. 2?

Symonds epitomises the Aussie spirit. It will be them vs the rest in the ICC Trophy.

RECENT comment announcing the demise of Australian cricket appears to be premature at best, wishful thinking at worst. Sure, England's star is in the ascendant and India has been very competitive in recent Test series with Australia but no one has the all-round strength of the Australians in both forms of the game.

As we have seen in the NatWest Trophy over the past week, India is struggling and will miss Sachin Tendulkar's brilliance and experience in the Champions Trophy tournament while England is struggling in the limited over version of the game, period. Without Flintoff in the last NatWest clash with India, England looked positively anaemic. They will need to go back to the drawing board before the Champions Trophy or they are likely to appear in the also-ran category at the business end of the tournament.

Two players who are barom-poorly with his Test match stats but it is rapidly looking like it could become terminal if he doesn't shake himself out of his current torpor. He reminds me somewhat of Michael Slater who, as a natural ball striker, tried to become even more aggressive in one-day cricket and finally lost his way completely for a period. Michael resurfaced in Tests as a pale shadow of his former self before stuttering into oblivion.

Schwag appears to be more mentally robust than Slater was but he would need to find himself soon or he might start to doubt himself as Slater did. More than anything else, he needs to define a role for himself in the shorter version of the game. He became an opener for one-day cricket and I believe it suits his personality and his style but he needs to use the same approach to batting in these matches as he does in Test cricket. His batting, while explosive in Tests, appears to have a measurement to it that is not as evident in limited-overs matches.

Fig. 4.4: *A provocative question headline used by* Outlook *to spark reader interest.*

One such headline was written about the advantages and disadvantages of foreign direct investment (FDI). The writer defended as well as attacked the virtues and ill effects of FDI. Instead of going for a bland headline, the writer chose the question mark format.

Label headline: **The pluses and minuses of FDI**
Better headline: **How dangerous can FDI be?**

Use Sparingly

A question headline must be used sparingly if it has to have impact. Too many question headlines will turn off the reader. Also, the surprise element of using a loaded question as a headline will be lost. In many newsrooms question headlines are considered to be a lazy way of addressing an issue. Juniors are advised to rewrite the question headlines.

Such an approach makes sense. For instance, the following headline about POTA detenus who had neither money nor links to important people could easily have been written without a question mark.

Original
No champions for non-VIP POTA detenus?
Revised
No one to take care of non-VIP POTA detenus

98

Another question headline in the same genre was written on the story that spoke about the growing differences between the Telangana Rashtriya Samiti and the Congress (Fig. 4.5). It could have easily been rewritten without a question mark as:

Congress, TRS differences growing

Fig. 4.5: *A question headline used in the* New Indian Express *that could easily have been written without a question mark.*

NUMBER HEADLINES

Numerals perform two major functions in a headline. The first is purely functional; the second is creative. The functional role is easy to define. It comes from the fact that numbers are used as adjectives in a headline. They inform the readers about the number of deaths, the losses incurred by a company, the number of cars sold in a year, the amount of money spent by ministers on foreign jaunts, etc.

The creative role springs from the interpretation of numbers. A simple number may be given a new life or spin by relating it creatively to an issue. For instance, a headline may state in a matter of fact manner that 15 people were killed in accidents involving Blueline buses in Delhi during a month. The same number can capture more attention if the headline states that one Delhite was killed every second day by Blueline buses.

The following are some important points that must be kept in mind while using numbers in headlines.

Numbers as Numerals

Numbers should be used as numerals in headlines since this saves space.

Use: **25 killed in Andhra bus accident**
Avoid: **Twenty-five killed in Andhra bus accident**

However, this is not a limiting condition. A number can be spelt out if it helps to balance a headline.

Avoid: **4 killed in**
             Kolkata blaze
Use: **Four killed in**
             Kolkata blaze

The second headline is more visually pleasing since the two decks are equal.

Numbers as Words

Numbers running into five digits and above should be used in words.

Use: **Karnataka gets Rs 50 crore grant**
Avoid: **Karnataka gets Rs 5,000,000,000 grant**

Use of Decimals

The decimals can be dropped in a headline when they form part of a large number.

Use: **Rs 538 crores paid as compensation to Kerala factory**
Avoid: **Rs 538.13 crores paid as compensation to Kerala factory**

It is not essential that a headline should state the last rupee and paisa that the factory got as compensation. The figure should be rounded off to the nearest digit in lakhs or crores.

Do not Use Fractions

Fractions should not be used in headlines. These disturb the visual harmony of the page.

Creative Use of Numbers

Numbers should not be looked upon as mere physical entities alone. They have a second and more important role to play. This relates to creativity and their intelligent use. Good headline writers use numbers to add new meaning or a new dimension to a headline. They may kill a headline if they fail to read meaning within numbers.

The release of MIT's list of bright young minds is a much-celebrated event in the US. The list names youngsters whom it expects to make a mark in select fields. The 2003 list had as many as 10 American students of Indian origin. This was a great reason for cheer in India as it showed how well Indians, and their descendants, are doing in the US. Unfortunately, the headline that was written did not do justice to the occasion. It said flatly:

10 of Indian origin in MIT's Technology Review 100

The point that every tenth name on that list was that of an Indian-American was glossed over. The headline would have grabbed more attention if it read:

Every 10th bright spark in MIT list is of Indian origin

Use of Casualty Figures

How does one write headlines about disasters where the early leads speak of estimated casualties? This invariably happens with natural or man-made calamities. In all these cases, it takes time to establish the number of people who have died.

The first lead speaks of people presumed killed or feared dead. The headline writer therefore faces the dilemma of stating with certainty that 20 people have died or wait till the final casualty figures are computed. The best policy is to qualify the casualty figure with an adjective. It is always advisable to err on the safe side. This improves the credibility of a newspaper. There is no point in stating that 50 persons have died in a train crash and then stating the final casualty figure the following day as 35.

In the following report about a boat tragedy the headline writer did the right thing by using the adjective feared in the headline.

30 feared dead as bus plunges into river

CHAMOLI: At least 30 people were feared dead when a state roadways bus fell into the raging Alaknanda river about 30 km from here this evening.

The bus was carrying 43 passengers, but the police and divers have so far recovered only 20 bodies.

According to police, the bus was negotiating a sharp curve when the tragedy occurred. Eyewitnesses fear that the toll may be much higher as the fierce current washed the bus away.

The same principle should be used for riot stories. The headline writer must exercise more caution in such stories. Most riot stories give two figures; one, the official toll provided by police authorities and two, the casualty figures spread by rumour mongers. The second figure is always higher than the one released by the authorities.

The reporters save their necks by using both the figures; of course, they qualify the second with the adjective unofficial sources. The headline writers now have to decide which toll figure to use, the official or the unofficial one. There are pitfalls in both. The rivals may scoop the newspaper by using a higher figure, and the headline writer will be pulled up for being too cautious. In the reverse situation the non-official figures being bandied about may turn out to be too high.

The best policy once again is to use the official figures. The newspaper is first reporting a fact provided by a government official, and second, it is being responsible. It is not inflaming passion by giving information that may be incorrect. There is no shame in erring on the wrong side while reporting riot deaths. The newspapers are in the business of reporting facts, and not scooping their rivals by reporting high and exaggerated figures.

EDITORIAL HEADLINE

The most sacrosanct page in a newspaper is the editorial. Its value can be gauged from the fact that the editors themselves supervise the running of this page. Each item on this page is sacred. But the page's ruling deities are the two editorials or leaders. Some newspapers use three editorials, while a few restrict themselves to a single editorial.

Great attention is paid to the writing of the editorial and the editorial headline. And why not? The editorial reflects the newspaper's opinion on issues of national importance, and is written by the most qualified and experienced staff on the rolls of a newspaper. Any mistake in the editorial or the editorial headline amounts to sacrilege.

There are two formats adopted by newspapers for the editorial headlines. The *Hindu* runs a single-deck format (Fig. 4.6), which is used both as a headline and comment; the *Times of India* (Fig. 4.7) has adopted a format where comment is used as a strapline.

AN EXPERIMENT IN DEMOCRACY

THE FIRST PRESIDENTIAL election in Afghanistan's history is back on course with the candidates contesting against the incumbent Hamid Karzai giving up their demand for the polls to be annulled. Mr. Karzai's 15 rivals alleged that the election had been vitiated by widespread malpractices and declared that they would boy-

that the incumbent would cross the 50 per cent mark, which he needs to do if a run-off with the second placed candidate is to be avoided. The nominee of the Northern Alliance and main challenger, Younis Qanooni, had hoped he would be able to persuade the other candidates to withdraw from the race so that he could con-

Fig. 4.6: *The editorial headline format adopted by the* Hindu.

Disinvest Mantris

The best way to change PSUs is to say 'No, Minister'

While Manmohan Singh goes on a roadshow to sell India as an investment destination in Britain and the US, heavy industry *mantri* Santosh Mohan Deb begins to question Suzuki's plans to invest about $200 million in a new plant in India. What kind of Jekyll and Hyde manoeuvre is this? Deb's ministry controls 18% government stake in India's

Fig. 4.7: *The editorial headline format adopted by the* Times of India.

The editorial headline, till recently, was the only headline where the newspaper allowed comment to be used. The comment or advice is put out boldly in the main headline, in the strapline, or in both. It reflects the stand taken by newspapers on major issues.

Here is an example of comment used by the *Times of India* for an editorial written on Foreign Direct Investment.

Main headline: **Clear the Clutter**
Strapline: **Don't let vested interests hijack FDI policy**

HEADLINES FOR LETTERS

A very important section in the newspaper is the Letters to the Editor column. It allows readers to express their opinion on contemporary issues. For long the headlines written for the letters were label headlines. They would just state the subject of the letter, without amplifying the reader's grievance or opinion. This was also because the space allocated for writing the headline was not enough. Here are some samples of headlines written for letters.

College Road
Traffic lights
Civic woes

The editors handling letters are more imaginative now. They want the column to be as readable as the news sections. There is also the realization that most letter writers are seeking action and the headlines therefore must capture this emotion. Some of the bolder headlines being written today are:

Don't go by the rules
Learn the lesson
Punish the babu
Fix the roads

However, it is still early days. It will take much more time for headlines of letters to get a definite personality.

CHAPTER HIGHLIGHTS

When to use quotes	*Quotes that need attribution*
1. When a news report is built on a quote.	1. Comments made by celebrities like film stars or politicians.
2. When the quote is controversial.	2. Quotes based on reports of committees, panels, etc.
3. When the quote brings in a dash of colour.	3. Quotes made by ministers, officials.
4. When it brings out emotions.	4. Quotes where the context needs to be brought out.

How to edit quotes

1. Articles and auxiliary verbs can be dropped in headlines.
2. Ellipsis should be used when two different quotes are joined together.
3. Irrelevant words can be dropped as long as the meaning is not affected.

Role and limitation of question headlines

1. Evoke curiosity.
2. Allow newspaper to skirt sensitive issues.
3. Useful for speculative stories.
4. Should be used sparingly.
5. Overuse reduces impact.

How to use numbers in headlines

1. Numerals should be used in place of numbers.
2. Numbers that run over five digits should be spelt out.
3. Decimal values should not be used in large numbers.
4. Fractions should not be used in headlines.
5. Whenever possible, numbers should be used intelligently to add meaning to a headline.

Role of editorial headlines

1. Give advice.
2. Suggest solutions.
3. Comment on issues.

Headlines for letters

1. Largely label heads.
2. Some comment can be seen now.

HEADLINE EXERCISES

Quotes in Headlines

Exercise 1

Go through one week's newspapers and locate five headlines where a quote has been used. Write the headline again using indirect speech.

Exercise 2

Go through one week's newspapers and identify five headlines where a quote has been paraphrased and the subject's name used as attribution. Write the headline as a direct quote.

Exercise 3

Write headlines for the five interviews that follow using the given headline parameters:

Point size: 30
Case: Upper-lower
Number of letters per column: 5
Column width: 4
Number of decks: 2

Interview 1

The following interview of Mr Sushil Kumar Shinde, the Chief Minister of Maharashtra, was published in the *Week* in the issue dated 7 September 2003.

Q. How do you view the latest of a series of blasts in eight months?
A. They are clearly intended to destabilise the state. The state's debt burden of Rs 93,000 crore is going down, the economy is improving, and tourism is looking up, with hotels reporting full occupancy. Several international giants have made huge investments in the state in the last few months. These terrorist acts are intended to sabotage the state's fast-track developmental activities.

Q. Many feel that Mumbai is on its way to becoming another Jerusalem. Are these fears justified?
A. Terrorism is a global phenomenon today. The attacks in Mumbai are a cause for national concern, particularly since the city is the centre of the country's trade and business. The police are doing their job to ensure that attacks do not recur.

Q. The opposition has demanded your government's dismissal.
A. The opposition should stand united with the government in such critical times. Such things can only further destabilise the state. The Congress has never resorted to such narrow politics either at the state or at the central level.

Q. There are fears among minorities that terrorist activities could foment communal disturbances, particularly as Assembly elections are approaching.
A. The government will ensure nobody gets the opportunity to create communal disturbances of any kind.

Q. There are intelligence reports indicating possibility of more blasts in the near future. Is the government aware of them?
A. No, but I will alert the persons concerned to take measures to prevent any such terrorist acts.

Interview 2

The following interview is of Ms Vasundhara Raje, who led the BJP to victory in the 2003 Rajasthan Assembly elections. The interview was published in the *Week* in the issue dated 14 December 2003.

Q. What next?
A. Good governance, obviously.

Q. Were you confident of winning by a huge margin?
A. Yes, I was quite sure of both victory as well as the margin though many of my colleagues didn't share my level of optimism.

Q. Do you think an anti-incumbency vote helped you win?
A. It was more of a pro-development vote in our favour, a kind of faith in our abilities to deliver.

Q. What are your priorities?
A. Tourism, industries, agriculture and relief to people in every manner possible.

Q. As the first woman chief minister of Rajasthan, can women expect anything special from you?
A. Women are my strength; 61 per cent of them have voted for me. I will make Rajasthan a haven for women empowerment and development.

Interview 3

The following interview of actress Preity Zinta was moved by Indo-Asian News Service on 12 September 2004 and was used by several publications.

Q. On the surface, *Dil Ne Jise Apna Kaha* looks like just another love story.
A. A-ha! Looks can be deceptive. Mine is a very sweet role. The whole film has a very nice flavour. It's very sensitive...Yeah, I really liked my role, and the film. I can't tell you more about my role because that would give away the plot. But when people see it they'd know it isn't just another sweet candyfloss film.

Anyway I couldn't say no to Salman Khan and Atul Agnihotri...Of course, I did the film for them. But I wouldn't have done it if I didn't like my role and the film.

Q. How was it working with Salman again?
A. The comfort level on the sets was very high. It was a very chilled set. Doing the film was a cakewalk. So yeah, personal relations do reflect on your profession. It was so stress-free. Salman and I had done *Chori Chori Chupke Chupke* and *Har Dil Jo Pyar Karega* earlier.

Dil Ne Jise... is the only film I've done with a co-star for the third time. There was Saif...but he wasn't opposite me in *Dil Chahta Hai*. So in a way Salman and I have grown together as actors. Salman is himself with me. He never tries to be a prankster or a gentleman when I'm around. We're just ourselves with one another.

Q. Do you share screen space with Bhoomika Chawla?

A. She has her own space and a very, very nice role that she has performed very well. Yeah, I do have scenes with her. She's a very sweet girl and a good actress. Don't look for signs of strain and stress here. Like I said this is a stress-free film. I must add Atul Agnihotri is a very capable director.

Q. You've so far been very lucky for first-time directors like Farhan Akhtar and Nikhil Advani.

A. Have I? But not for Honey Aunty (Honey Irani directed *Armaan*). I hope I prove lucky for Atul. He really deserves to succeed. I don't think anyone will feel cheated after seeing *Dil Ne Jise Apna Kaha*. Everyone will come out with a smile. And also, the film gives off a very positive message. Cinema does have a huge influence on people's minds. I hope this one makes a difference.

Interview 4

The following interview of NASSCOM President, Mr Kiran Karnik, was published in the *Week* in the issue dated 19 September 2004.

Q. Is there a feeling in the IT sector that Bangalore is slipping as the IT capital of India?

A. Yes and no. Bangalore continues to be predominant in terms of the size, exports and potential of the IT industry. There is concern about the straining infrastructure. A lot needs to be done to improve it considering that some other cities have more infrastructure. This is not a crisis because there are new people continuing to go to Bangalore. I would compare Bangalore to the Indian cricket team. It is like losing three quick wickets when the team is on the verge of victory. Instead of accelerating, it seems to be slowing down.

Q. But infrastructure problems in Bangalore existed even when S.M. Krishna was chief minister.

A. The gap between the demand-supply (of infrastructure) has widened. We should not be drawing comparisons with other states, but with cities worldwide.

The infrastructure in China is ahead of the industry's needs. It is the other way around here: you start thinking of infrastructure after the companies come here. Earlier, the gap between demand and supply was not so large in Bangalore. There were no water or power problems. Over the years, the demands of the industry are becoming more sophisticated.

Earlier, you ran a software company using generators. Now, every shortfall creates a crisis. If one employee comes in late, he cannot integrate with the team he is working with.

Q. What, do you feel, is the most glaring infrastructure problem in Bangalore?

A. Public transport. They have to think about a mass transport system. They have been speaking about an elevated light rail system and a metro for the last 10 years, but there has been no action. There is no dynamism. There is nobody who says, 'Let's do it now.'

Q. Have foreign investors expressed concern over the infrastructure?

A. Very much so. What happened to that great international airport in Bangalore? Foreign investors whisper, 'Have you seen the Shanghai Airport?'

For foreign direct investment and for Indian companies that want to expand, such factors put a brake on their plans. We have to ask ourselves whether we are going to be standing in a traffic jam three years from now.

Interview 5

The following interview of cricketer Rahul Dravid was published in the *Week* in the issue dated 28 December 2003. The interview was conducted after a great innings from the stylish batsman that helped India win a test in Australia.

Q. What did Sourav say when he came and hugged you?
A. He said well done! The hugging was intense because I have been playing an active part in rebuilding this team. Moments like this win are a very important part of the process and we both knew that. The victory reinforced our belief that we were on the right path [of making this team into the best], and we are getting there.

Q. Did you set some goals for yourself before the series?
A. I told myself to just get here and play good cricket. In the last tour I had planned so well in advance. I didn't do it this time. All I told myself was to get used to the conditions as early as possible and play good cricket.

Q. Did you think you were in the 'zone' while you were batting in the match?
A. I don't think so. I have never experienced the feeling before. But there were stages in the match when I felt really in control of the situation. I think I slipped in and out of phases out there.

Q. Which innings was more difficult — the first one where 556 stared out at you or the second, chasing a small target?
A. The first was very important for us to remain in the game and it helped us to do that. But the second was far more difficult because there was the pressure of finishing the job.

Q. What were you thinking before going out to bat in the second innings?
A. I believed right from the morning of the last day that we would win the match. We all had a strong feeling about it. I knew that if not me someone else was going to do it come what may.

Q. Would you consider the current phase of your batting your best?
A. Yes. Starting from the series against the West Indies two years ago. I feel so comfortable with myself while batting, and relaxed. I trust my game; it's not like I have done anything special with my technique. I guess it's about maturing. Experience teaches you and you tend not to repeat mistakes often.

Exercise 4

Write headlines for the five news reports that follow:

a. By using partial quotes.
b. By using attribution.

The headline parameters are as follows:
a. For partial quotes
Point size: 30
Case: Upper-lower
Number of letters per column: 5
Column width: 5
Number of decks: 1

b. For headlines with attribution
Point size: 24
Case: Upper-lower
Number of letters per column: 7
Column width: 2
Number of decks: 2

News Report 1

MUMBAI (IANS): Aishwarya Rai firmly brushes off rumours about her signing a new film with Salman Khan saying that is "out of the question".

As clear and focused about her principles and priorities as ever, Ash brushes off speculation doing the rounds about her doing a film with Salman. "Working with Salman is out of the question. And you can quote me on that."

"When I wrote out that press statement stating what I had to about the end of all association with him, I was in hospital with a fractured foot. I wrote that statement from my hospital bed where I had lots of time to think about what I was doing," Aishwarya Rai told IANS in an interview.

"I'm not the kind of person who'd reverse her decision to suit her purposes. The question of going back on my words just doesn't arise. Come on! I let go of the chance of working with Sanjay Leela Bhansali just to stand by my convictions. Why would I change my mind for a lesser film?" Aishwarya reasons.

News Report 2

BANGALORE (ENS): V.S. Naipaul expressed surprise over the observation that a lot of youngsters identified with his writings, especially in rural areas, during a book launch session in Bangalore.

"All my writing life, I was under the impression that I don't have much of an audience. But I feel happy with the revelation," he quipped.

When a fan pointed out that none of his novels had a great man-woman relationship, Naipaul looked thunderstruck and quickly rose in defence, "I don't agree with that. Even in my latest novel, there is a profound man-woman relationship. Maybe not the M&B way."

The author spoke about the power of change in society and felt that things change because people want them to. On a serious note he said, "I find many things disturbing, like the technological civilisation living in low popular culture. What happened in Iraq was shameful. People find it hard to realise that their civilisation is slowly decaying. I am a writer who is trying to understand the world he lives in."

And as always, his passing shot was faultless. When queried whether 56 is too old an age to write a novel, Sir Naipaul said, "Yes, It's the right age to pen an autobiography."

News Report 3

MUMBAI (UNI): To woo the Indian tourists and entertainment industry, New Zealand is singing the tune of 'Kaho Na Pyaar Hai' to Bollywood movie makers.

Interestingly, the New Zealand Prime Minister, Ms Helen Clark, who is visiting India, herself has taken the initiative to promote her country. She felicitated noted director Rakesh Roshan, actor Hrithik Roshan and actress Amisha Patel for their contribution in showcasing New Zealand to India through their superhit film *Kaho Na Pyaar Hai* here last evening.

"Over 100 Bollywood movies had been filmed in the scenic backdrop of New Zealand in last five years. And many more Hindi movies are expected to shoot at the various locations of New Zealand."

She informed that the number of Indian tourists visiting New Zealand had grown manifold after the 1999 spectacular success of *Kaho Na Pyaar Hai*.

"New Zealand Government wanted to acknowledge the part played by the makers of *Kaho Na Pyaar Hai* in promoting the country as the international tourist destination. The country was very much there in the script of the film and the location was so close to the story."

New Zealand has also turned to an international film-making destination with significant Hollywood films shot there. The Academy Award winning *The Lord of the Rings*, directed by New Zealander Peter Jackson, has given boost to this trend.

Current film productions underway in New Zealand include *The Lion, The Witch* and *The Wardrobe and King Kong*.

She said besides having a superb line-up of technology companies and a dynamic local film industry, New Zealand also offers a host of natural advantages which position it as a first choice for overseas film, television and commercial productions.

"These include an unspoilt, diverse and easily accessible landscape, a temperate climate, and high sunshine hours," she said.

News Report 4

NEW DELHI (PTI): Lauding the killing of forest brigand and notorious sandalwood smuggler Veerappan, the Centre today said with his death the symbol of 'unlawfulness' has been eliminated.

"We appreciate the action taken. He (Veerappan) symbolised unlawfulness and with this (killing), the symbol has also been eliminated," Union Home Minister Shivraj Patil said here.

He said Tamil Nadu, Karnataka and Central forces had initiated action and the government appreciates their achievement.

Asked how the government was planning to deal with rest of Veerappan's associates, Patil said it was not an issue of killing them but rather arresting and putting them behind bars.

"The process is already on and we will provide them whatever central assistance, they want," Patil added.

News Report 5

NEW DELHI (PTI): CT Scan comes with a capital 'C' (Caution) as latest research says the risk of dying by cancer increases every time a person undergoes a Computed Tomography (CT) examination.

"For a person of 45 years, this cancer risk is 0.08 per cent—odds of 1 in 1250—a small percentage, but still the risk is cumulative and depends on age," says David J Brenner, a radiation oncologist at Columbia University in the latest issue of *Radiology*.

The researchers estimated that if the same 45-year-old person undergoes the examination every year for the next 30 years his risk of dying by cancer is about two per cent—one in 50. Thus, if 50 people of 45 years undergo CT tests annually for the next 30 years, one of them may die of cancer induced by the radiation dose received.

However, Dr K S Parthasarthy, former secretary, Atomic Energy Regulatory Board, Mumbai, says, "The benefits of a clinically indicated CT scan far exceed the harm from it. But some specialists carry out CT scan indiscriminately."

He says the AERB sent various do's and don'ts on doing CT in children to most of the clinics in the country, but a preliminary survey indicated that "many installations ignore such suggestions".

"CT makes it possible to diagnose certain diseases earlier and more accurately than with other imaging tools. So what is needed is optimised and judicious use of the technology," says Dr Yatish Agarwal, a radiologist at Safdarjung Hospital.

QUESTION HEADLINES

Exercise 1

Go through one month's newspapers to locate five question headlines. Rewrite each headline to remove the question mark.

Exercise 2

Write a question headline for the three news reports that follow using the given headline parameters. Also, use the same parameters to write a headline without a question mark.

Point size: 30
Case: Upper-lower
Number of letters per column: 5
Column width: 5
Number of decks: 1

News Report 1

JAIPUR (IANS): A 500-year-old donkey fair that used to draw buyers from as far as Afghanistan is slowly losing its appeal, and, at this rate, may even die.

Held every year at Looniyawas, about 20 km from here, the donkey fair used to be the largest in Asia. But it is little more than a state-level fair today.

"We used to get buyers from as far as Afghanistan and places like Ladakh, (other places in) Jammu and Kashmir and Uttar Pradesh," Ummed Singh Rajawat, president of the organisation that holds the fair, told IANS.

"But thanks to mechanisation, no one from farther than Gujarat or Haryana visits us now."

The three-day fair ended on Saturday. Around 2,500 animals took part, but it is no more an exclusively donkey affair. More than a quarter of the participants were horses and mules.

Murari, a trader from Jamnagar in Gujarat, also blamed increased use of tractors and motor vehicles for the declining interest in donkeys.

"I have been attending this fair for more than 10 years. Earlier, business used to be brisk with a rush of buyers and sellers. But for three or four years, it has become really dull. The number of participants has also gone down," he says.

The prices of donkeys have also fallen.

"Earlier, a donkey used to sell for around Rs. 10,000–12,000 ($220–260). Now it is hard to find a buyer even for Rs. 5,000 ($110)," Rajawat says.

News Report 2

AGRA (IANS): The Taj Mahal, India's biggest tourist draw, might already be tilting and may even crumble or sink if the government does not restore its original ecological settings.

Two noted historians have warned that the bed of the river Yamuna must be re-filled with water if the world's most famous monument, built on its banks, is to be saved.

The Taj Mahal is celebrating its 350th anniversary this year. Built with high quality white marble, it came up in the 17th century and is known as the monument of love.

"Dangerous tilts in its minarets, first noticed as early as 1942 and mentioned in various reports, have continued to increase over the years. They are caused by the dry river bed," Ram Nath, a former head of Rajasthan University's history department, told IANS.

"The river forms an integral part of the monument's design. All available historical records indicate that the Yamuna was always full of water and extensively used for transport. Even Shahjahan's (the Mughal king who built the monument) body was brought to the Taj from the Agra Fort in a boat," he said.

Agam Prasad Mathur, a former vice chancellor of Agra University, agreed.

"Yamuna used to be full of water to maintain the monument's balance and absorb tectonic shocks. Now that the river bed is dry, the Taj is exposed to the elements," he said.

Both historians said the government must focus on preserving the monument instead of just exploiting its tremendous tourist appeal.

"And if the Taj is to be preserved for posterity, the Yamuna must be rescued first," they added.

News Report 3

BANGALORE (ENS): When truth is unavailable, speculation takes over. In Bangalore, as it must be in Coimbatore and Salem and Chennai, the air is thick with rumours of how forest brigand Veerappan so uncharacteristically walked into a police trap.

A dozen versions are already circulating. According to one, emanating from circles linked to the police, a Tamil Nadu-based person, who played a key role in the release of actor Rajkumar, is suspected to have led Veerappan into the STF trap on Monday night.

The police always persecuted this man for his alleged links with Veerappan even after he facilitated Dr Rajkumar's release from jungles.

One version suggests that the men planted in Veerappan's gang were his boys. This was believable as they were familiar to the poacher's gang and had visited the hideouts several times before.

It was never easy to fool Veerappan—those who attempted perished without a trace before. He was known not to trust his own shadow. It is difficult to believe the police claims here that an STF plant won over the poacher in the last few months, and he came out of his hideout with all the members of his gang.

The way the entire gang travelled in the van along with some cash suggests that they could be changing their hideout as the gang frequently did. That the gang also carried weapons lends credence to this.

The gangster was never known to have sugar or eyesight problems. In fact, his sharp eyesight was folklore in the region. He, however, had asthma but never had any leg pain as some police claims go. He would walk for 20 km at a stretch in forests with ration and weapon tugged on his shoulders.

Assume for a moment that Veerappan was moving out for treatment. In that case, why would he take his entire team along—something he was never known to do unless he was shifting his lair.

But why would this key man, whom the poacher trusted for years, double-cross? He could have done it for a quid pro quo.

Number Headlines

Exercise 1

Go through last month's newspapers and locate five headlines that have made an imaginative use of numbers.

Exercise 2

Write two headlines for each of the following three news reports. In the first headline, the numbers can be used as simple, straight units. In the second the numbers should be used creatively to add value to the headline. The headlines should be written using the following parameters:

Point size: 30
Case: Upper-lower
Number of letters per column: 5
Column width: 5
Number of decks: 1

News Report 1

NEW DELHI (UNI): The popular demand for rationalisation of the fares of Shatabdi and Rajdhani Express trains seems to hold ground specially in view of the fact that only 4 out of a total of 26 Shatabdis and 10 out of 38 Rajdhanis figure among the 100 most frequently travelled trains in the country.

The Shatabdis being run as the elite superfast trains in the country are popular but not to the extent as the Railways ideally would have expected these to be. Similar is the case with Rajdhanis but the fare and other factors do not allow lower and lower middle class to really adopt these trains despite fairly decent runs of these trains.

Indian Railways run 26 (13 pairs) Shatabdis which mainly link all the Capital cities but only four—New Delhi-Lucknow, New Delhi-Dehradun, New Delhi-Chennai and New Delhi-Bangalore have caught the fancy of the passengers in a big way. These four Shatabdis are the ones which got mention in the list of 100 most popular trains, according to the railways website.

News Report 2

NEW DELHI (PTI): Reflecting the pressures of debt, the government will spend the largest share of 23 paise from every rupee earned in 2004–05 for paying interest on its borrowings.

Incidentally, 24 paisa of every budget rupee that the government will get will be through borrowings, according to the Union budget for 2004–05, presented by Finance Minister P. Chidambaram on Thursday.

Other non-plan expenditure eats away 11 paisa of every rupee earned while subsidy burden is to the extent of 8 paisa. Fourteen paisa out of every rupee would go towards meeting the defence outlay while 16 paisa has been allocated for the Central plan.

States' share of taxes and duties is 15 paisa in every rupee and their share of plan assistance is 10 paisa. Non-plan assistance to states and Union Territory governments takes away the remaining 3 paisa in every rupee.

On the receipt side, income tax gives only 9 paisa in every rupee while corporate tax contributes 16 paisa. Customs duties give 10 paisa of every rupee and excise chip in 19 paisa. Other taxes give 3 paisa in every rupee.

Non-debt capital receipts stand at 6 paisa and non-tax revenue at 13 paisa.

News Report 3

LONDON (Reuters): Women still hit a glass ceiling in the board rooms of some of the world's largest companies even though they have made some strides at executive levels, according to a study.

Though women in the United States say the sense of tokenism is fading, and there are far more women with directorships than there used to be, there is still a long way to go around the world.

A study of the Fortune Magazine Global 200 companies by Corporate Women Directors International (CWDI) showed the percentage of women directors was 10.4 per cent or 285 board seats held by women out of 2,751 possible seats.

The study showed the United States led the world with women comprising 17.5 per cent of the boards of the 78 US companies reviewed, but other countries lagged. In France, for example, women accounted for 7.2 per cent of board members in 10 companies, and in Japan 0.7 per cent of board members of 27 companies were women.

EDITORIAL HEADLINES

Exercise 1

Go through the editorials published in last week's newspapers and locate the headline that you liked most. Give reasons for selecting the headline.

Exercise 2

Write a headline for each of the following three editorials published in the *New Indian Express*, making sure that the headline is prescriptive or advisory. The headline should be written using the following parameters:

Main headline

Point size: 28

Case: Upper-lower

Number of letters per column: 6

Column width: 2

Number of decks: 1

Strapline

Point size: 14

Case: Upper-lower

Number of letters per column: 14

Column width: 2

Number of decks: 1

Editorial 1

It happened one September in 1987. By one account, in the environs of Deorala, a village in Rajasthan's Sikar district, the sale of coconuts suddenly shot up. Aware that the coconut is a customary offering at religious rites but clueless about any impending holy day, the local police reportedly did a bit of snooping. And chanced upon a horrendous scene in Deorala. A teenaged widow had been burned at her husband's pyre, the legend of Roop

Kanwar had been created and thousands of worshippers were flocking to the duly designated Sati sthal. Calendar art had taken ghoulish colours, and prints of Roop Kanwar amidst the flames, with her husband's corpse on her lap, were selling briskly. The cops' Sherlock Holmes take may be rather simplistic, but as news of the death spread, the battlelines were drawn. Twentieth century Indians shuddered at the perpetration of such inhuman practices. A new, never mind how defective, law was passed by Parliament and dozens of persons were booked for abetting and glorifying the sati. Some orthodox vigilantes may have banded together in groups like the Dharam Rakshak Samiti, but the feeling was that modern India had once again reiterated its commitment to modernity and gender equality.

It's time to amend that narrative. It seems that 17 years later, we cannot be quite certain that there was even a case of sati recorded in Deorala! Last week a special Jaipur court let off 11 persons accused of glorifying sati in the wake of Kanwar's death. The prosecution, said the court, had failed to conclusively establish that an act of sati had in fact occurred at Deorala, September 1987; hence the question of them glorifying it did not arise.

How very apt it all is. It took just days, perhaps hours, for Roop Kanwar's death to pass into the realm of mythology. An act of murder was almost instantaneously recast as supernatural intervention—with stories circulating about the 18 year old ascending the pyre and raising her hand and the pyre lighting itself in response. Deorala was a key test for India. It highlighted the prevalence of savage rites, it reflected the sorry status of women. It focussed civil society on the rites and practices crying for reform. Who could have thought then that less than two decades later we'd instead be struggling to establish that the sati had actually occurred.

Editorial 2

The UPA's strategy for raising employment rests on very weak pillars. The weakest is the new slogan coined by Prime Minister Manmohan Singh: *rozgar badhao* (increase employment). It goes with an assurance not to bring in 'hire and fire' by changing labour laws. Labour laws may apply only to organised labour which constitute 7 per cent of the work force, but by keeping them in place India has already witnessed an incredibly slow growth in employment in large-scale industry. It is not surprising that investors are unwilling to take the risk of setting up industries which they will not be allowed to close down, or hire workers who they cannot fire. The slow growth of employment in the large-scale private manufacturing sector is a major contributor to the growth of unemployment in the country. Today, central and state governments are not in a position to increase employment significantly by more hiring. Therefore, the slogan that employment should be enhanced without a change in labour laws translates into saying that jobs in the unorganised sector should grow. But for these jobs to grow, the country needs growth.

The second pillar of the UPA's strategy to raise employment is the proposal to give 100 days per year of work to able-bodied rural job-seekers. In this case again there is an analytical mistake. Employment guarantee schemes, designed for coping with droughts, are being sought to be used to solve chronic problems. Unemployment is highest among the highly educated. NSSO data shows that in 1999–00, unemployment among illiterates was just 0.2 per cent. For those educated up to primary school, unemployment was 1.2 per cent. In contrast, unemployment among college graduates was 8.8 per cent. The employment guarantee scheme will not target employment where it is the highest. The pitiful resources of the government can hardly overcome economy-wide labour market issues. If there is a chronic problem in the labour market, a government job guarantee scheme can hardly address it. It is not the job of the government to give jobs. The job of the government is to create an environment where the economy grows well.

If India had succeeded in massive industrialisation, like China, this would have generated a great deal of employment, particularly for college graduates who would be technicians operating machines. This would have further created incentives for people to get education. If the government is serious about the unemployment problem, this is the area where a concerted policy focus is required. What India needs to do is to launch a concerted attack on matching China in the game of globalised production. This includes rationalisation of customs and excise and VAT, removal of small-scale sector reservations, easing FDI procedures, as well as reforms to labour law.

Editorial 3

The Centre's decision to wind up the Tehelka Commission, headed by Justice S.N. Phukan, raises serious questions about the sanctity of government-instituted commissions. It is another matter, of course, that these commissions have often been set up to tide over the immediate discomfort of a particular event or development, and that the reports of most commissions of inquiry have been treated cavalierly by the government of the day. Still, they do represent an impulse—not just of a party or government but of the nation—to correct serious anomalies in the system. They therefore demand a commitment that has, necessarily, to cut across party lines and rise above the sensitivities and interests of those in power.

Of course it is the prerogative of the government of the day to wind up a commission instituted by an earlier one—a point acknowledged by Justice Phukan himself—but the norm generally has been for new governments to allow commissions to carry on until a satisfactory conclusion to their exertions is reached. For instance, the Shiv Sena-BJP government's move to scuttle the Srikrishna Commission inquiry in 1996 proved so controversial that one of the decisions taken by the 13-day Atal Bihari Vajpayee government was, in fact, to reinstate it.

Union law minister, H.R. Bhardwaj, justified the move to wind up the Phukan inquiry by arguing that it was going nowhere. But how would he know this if the inquiry was not complete? Also, since Bhardwaj himself maintained that Justice Phukan had not exonerated George Fernandes in his interim report, is he right in presuming that the "various personalities" in the scam were not to come under the Commission's scanner? The point is not that the Tehelka expose does not demand serious institutional correctives since it involves not just murky defence deals, but ministerial impropriety and the financial misdemeanour of a senior BJP functionary. The point is that if the process in achieving this were to appear partisan, it would be a self-defeating exercise. A bipartisan approach to government inquiries is the best way to ensure institutional reform.

HEADLINES FOR LETTERS TO THE EDITOR

Exercise 1

Study the headline style used by the leading newspapers published in your city. Select any three headlines that you thought were inappropriate. Write them again giving reasons for your action.

Exercise 2

Write two headlines for each of the following three letters meant for publication in the Letters to the Editor column. The first headline should be a label headline. The second headline should be commentative. The headlines should be written using the following parameters:

Point size: 14
Case: Upper-lower
Number of letters per column: 14
Column width: 1

Letter 1

Sir, The chaos in Chennai train services caused by the 'inspection' tour of Lalu is not a surprise. What is more amusing is his deputy telling the journalists that the special train of his boss would disrupt the train schedule. When will our ministers learn to do their work without fanfare and without disturbing common man's life? That there were hardly any railway personnel available for informing the passengers about the arrival and departure of trains is because the railway officials were more interested in getting a good certificate from their political boss than serving the common man.

Koranad, Mumbai

Letter 2

Sir, I go to work on Old Mahabalipuram road. The entire drive from Tambaram to Old Mahabalipuram Road is a torture. The roads on first look seem fine but the reality is that they are a maze of patch-up work that has been done multiple times. Because of this there are numerous potholes and uneven surfaces. My car that was giving me excellent service and low maintenance in Hyderabad has started rattling within a year of coming to Chennai. So much for being a metro. I also wonder if contracts are given for doing patchwork. Or is it that the contracts are for relaying the roads but on the ground that only patchwork is done? The Velachery road and the road leading from Medavakkam to Old Mahabalipuram Road have not been tarred even once in the last one full year that I have been driving on them.

Pallavi, Chennai

Letter 3

Sir, The suicide of 14-year-old Vignaini raises many questions, especially as she blamed her class teacher for scolding her in front of boys. The incident should make school authorities to take note of teacher-student relationships. The parents too should advise their wards as to how they should deal with their teachers.

Teachers today have to be more sensitive. They must understand that some children have highly impressionable minds, and are emotionally unstable. They must handle them with sensitivity.

Anita Maheshwari, Lucknow.

5

HEADLINE PROPS

A report written in an inverted pyramid format pitchforks the most important news point to the top of the story. That is why nine out of 10 headlines are built on the news point enshrined in the lead. But there are several news reports that are built on more than one news point. This is especially true of developing or analytical stories. In such cases, headline writers have two options: one, focus on the point that is most important in their judgement; and two, use a headline prop to highlight other important points.

Headline props, as the name suggests, are supporting headlines. They provide the extra words and space that a headline writer desperately needs to make the headline more meaningful. Over the years, newspapers have evolved different kinds of headline props to suit their needs. These props come in different formats and serve different purposes. Interestingly, their role also differs from newspaper to newspaper. Broadly, they can be categorised as follows:

SHOULDER OR KICKER

A shoulder or kicker is the small headline that is placed on top of the main headline. Initially, it was used to highlight the subject of the story. Today, it is used to highlight news points too. However, the format remains the same; the shoulder continues to be written in a small point size. Also, its role remains unchanged; even today it supplements the main headline.

But what has changed is the thrust. The classic shoulders that highlighted the subject of the story have given way to description-based shoulders. Here too newspapers are quite fluid; they have modified the shoulders to meet different needs. A shoulder today can combine the subject of a story with a news point. A good example of such a hybrid shoulder was the one that was used in the *Hindu* (Fig. 5.1) in which the shoulder had two elements: cricket as the subject of the story and the good performance by Damien Martyn as the news point.

But the stress surely is to use the shoulder to underscore the news points. The *Asian Age* chose the shoulder to highlight the scores made by the top Indian batsmen, something that was unthinkable in the past (Fig. 5.2).

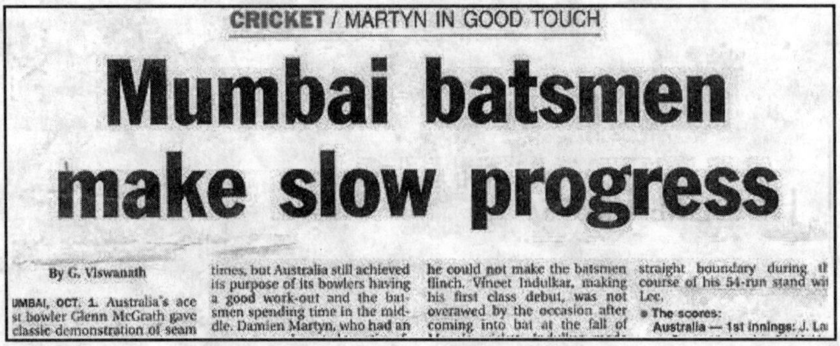

CRICKET / MARTYN IN GOOD TOUCH

Mumbai batsmen make slow progress

By G. Viswanath

UMBAI, OCT. 1. Australia's ace st bowler Glenn McGrath gave classic demonstration of seam

times, but Australia still achieved its purpose of its bowlers having a good work-out and the batsmen spending time in the middle. Damien Martyn, who had an

he could not make the batsmen flinch. Vineet Indulkar, making his first class debut, was not overawed by the occasion after coming into bat at the fall of

straight boundary during th course of his 54-run stand wit Lee.

● The scores:
Australia — 1st innings: J. La

Fig. 5.1: *A shoulder used by the* Hindu *for a sports story run at the top of the page. It is in a small point size and positioned on top of the main headline.*

CHOPRA 5, SEHWAG 0, SOURAV 5, LAXMAN 3

COME BACK, SACHIN

Fig. 5.2: *A shoulder used by the* Asian Age *to highlight the scores of the top Indian batsmen in a Test match against Australia in 2004.*

A similar stress on news points was noticed in the headlines that were written during the 2004 hostage crisis in which three Indians were among the seven drivers who were taken hostage by a group called The Holders of the Black Banner in Iraq. Three headlines that were used to report the unfolding events are reproduced here:

The *New Indian Express* used the shoulder to report two major news points.

Shoulder: **India makes contact; to meet negotiator today**
Main headline: **Iraq captors give**
24 more hours

The *Asian Age* used the shoulder to cover three major developments that took place on one day. These were: Kenya's claim that all seven hostages had been released, Delhi saying that it had no confirmation on the subject and the Iraqi negotiator announcing that he had decided to pull out. The main headline summed up the state of affairs—that the picture was far from clear.

Shoulder: **Kenya claims all 7 freed, Delhi says no confirmation;**
Negotiator pulls out
Main headline: **CONFUSION OVER HOSTAGES**

The *Hindu* too chose to summarize the situation by highlighting the uncertainty in the main headline. But only one point—that the negotiator had pulled out—was used as a shoulder.

Shoulder: **Mediator withdraws from talks**
Main headline: **Uncertainty over hostages release**

The shoulder is being used to perform one more task—to comment. The *Indian Express*, Mumbai, used the shoulder to raise a question mark about the killing of four members of a family in a Mumbai suburb.

Shoulder: **MURDER OR SUICIDE? Police find house bolted from outside, domestic help also found dead**
Main Headline: **Family found dead in Santa Cruz**

Shoulders are also being written as part of a read-in headline. In such cases, the shoulder is part of the main headline but written in a smaller point size. The *Hindu* used this format to report the statement made by the Prime Minister Dr Manmohan Singh to Left leaders regarding the use of foreign consultants in the Planning Commission (Fig. 5.3). However, the read-in headlines are not very popular, and are used sparingly.

MANMOHAN TELLS LEFT LEADERS

"We will devise mechanism for consultations"

By Our Special Correspondent

NEW DELHI, OCT.1. The Prime Minister, Manmohan Singh, in- for consultation.

On Thursday, the Planning Commission said it would revert to the earlier practice of consult-

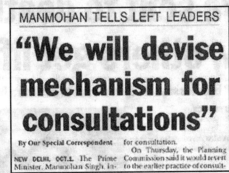

Fig. 5.3: *A shoulder that reads into the main headline.*

Interestingly, shoulders have become an important design tool also. Newspapers now set shoulders in reverse or against colour backgrounds to provide contrast on the page (Fig. 5.4).

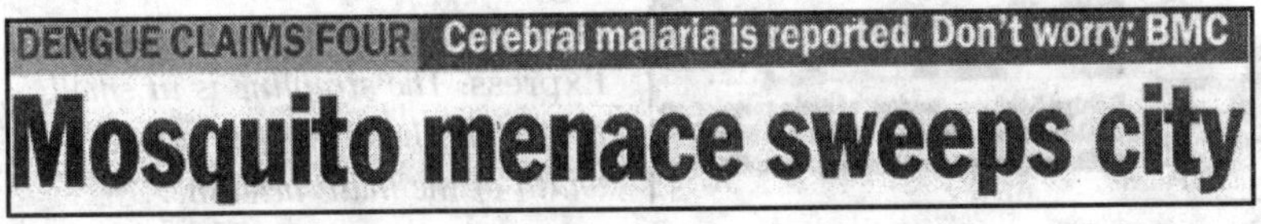
DENGUE CLAIMS FOUR Cerebral malaria is reported. Don't worry: BMC

Mosquito menace sweeps city

Fig. 5.4: *A shoulder used against a colour background in the* Indian Express.

However, despite their increased popularity and flexibility, newspapers do not encourage extensive use of shoulders. They invariably limit shoulders to a few stories because they want the headlines to stand on their own and not depend on props. They also do not want to waste space by using a shoulder over each headline. Another irritant that reduces the utility of the shoulder is the visual appeal. Too many shoulders make the page look cluttered.

STRAPLINE OR REVERSE SHOULDER

The strapline, also called reverse shoulder in some newspapers, is a more popular form of headline prop. It is run beneath the main headline and is used to enlarge or amplify the main news point. Once again there are no fixed rules regarding the use of straplines. They may highlight one point or several points. But what is certain is their location—beneath the main headline—and point size—smaller than the main headline (Fig. 5.5).

Design editors insist that the straplines should straddle the same width as the main headline since short straplines are not visually appealing. Sometimes they are run in one or two columns beneath the main headline. When run as a single column they are placed over the first paragraph, and should not be confused with blurbs (Fig. 5.6).

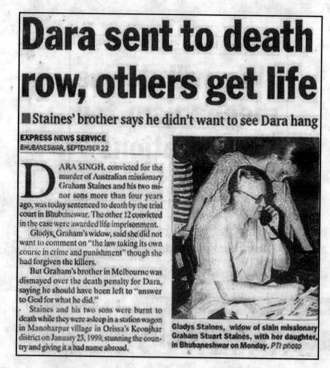

Fig. 5.5: *A strapline used in the Dara Singh case in the* Indian Express. *The strapline is in small points and has been run across the width of the main headline.*

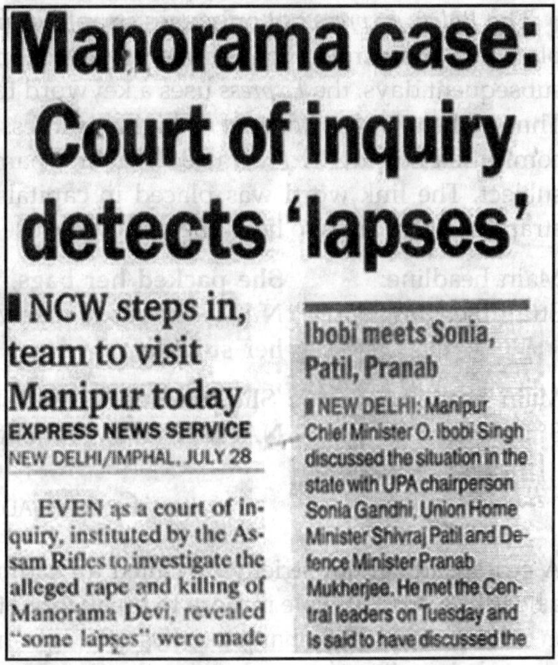

Manorama case: Court of inquiry detects 'lapses'

■ NCW steps in, team to visit Manipur today

EXPRESS NEWS SERVICE
NEW DELHI/IMPHAL, JULY 28

EVEN as a court of inquiry, instituted by the Assam Rifles to investigate the alleged rape and killing of Manorama Devi, revealed "some lapses" were made

Ibobi meets Sonia, Patil, Pranab

■ NEW DELHI: Manipur Chief Minister O. Ibobi Singh discussed the situation in the state with UPA chairperson Sonia Gandhi, Union Home Minister Shivraj Patil and Defence Minister Pranab Mukherjee. He met the Central leaders on Tuesday and is said to have discussed the

Fig. 5.6: *A strapline used in a single column format beneath the main headline.*

The point size used to write a strapline is always less than that of the main headline. This enables the reader to distinguish the main point of a news report from the supporting points. Like shoulders, straplines too are now set in reverse and against colour backgrounds (Fig. 5.7) to add to the page's visual appeal.

End of an 86-year-old curse

Baseball's perennial also-rans Red Sox pen new script with World Series success

Fig. 5.7: *A strapline used in reverse.*

Two newspapers that make liberal use of straplines are the *Indian Express* and the *Hindustan Times*. Both use it intelligently as extra hooks to draw readers into stories. They also use them to provide extra information to readers who skim headlines to learn the day's developments.

A good example of a strapline used by the *Indian Express* pertains to a sensex story. When the sensex rose by 40 points one day, the *Express* used this point as the main headline, and used a strapline to give the reason for the increase.

Main headline: **Sensex gains 40 points**
Reverse Shoulder: **Revival of monsoons and positive FII inflow has operators enlarging commitments**

The *Indian Express* not only uses straplines prolifically but has modified them to play one more role. For related news reports, published the same day or on subsequent days, the *Express* uses a keyword to indicate that the stories are related. Thus, when Nafisa Joseph, a highly successful model and former Miss India, committed suicide, *Express* used her first name 'Nafisa' to link all stories on the subject. The link word was placed in capitals to separate it from the rest of the strapline. Here are two headlines that were used in the *Express* on the tragic suicide:

Main headline:	**She packed her bags, was ready to leave**
Strapline:	**NAFISA: Was to marry next week, Mom blames fiance for her suicide**
Main headline:	**'She touched us with her grace, poise'**
Strapline:	**NAFISA: MTV colleague Cyrus Broacha recounts...**

CROSSHEADS

A crosshead cannot strictly be called a headline. But in many ways it works like a headline prop. Its role is more to break monotony and help sustain reader interest in a long story. The characteristics of a crosshead are:

(a) It is written in a point size that is generally two points more than the body type; sometimes it may be more than this.

(b) It is positioned in between the running text. The positioning may be flush left or centred.

(c) A crosshead is positioned after three to five paragraphs depending on the story display and newspaper style.

(d) It captures the most important news point mentioned in the paragraph or paragraphs over which it is positioned.

A crosshead serves two important purposes:

(a) It breaks the greyness of text especially if the story is quite deep.

(b) It gives the readers an idea of what to expect in the paragraphs that follow.

However, very few newspapers use crossheads in news stories today. One of the few newspapers that uses it quite regularly is the *Hindu* (Fig. 5.8). Newspapers mostly use it on the edit page, where there is virtually no illustration and the articles are quite deep.

SIDEHEAD

Strictly speaking, sidehead, like crosshead, cannot be considered a headline prop. However, it too functions like a headline prop. The main characteristics of a sidehead (Fig. 5.9) are:

(a) It is positioned at the start of a paragraph.

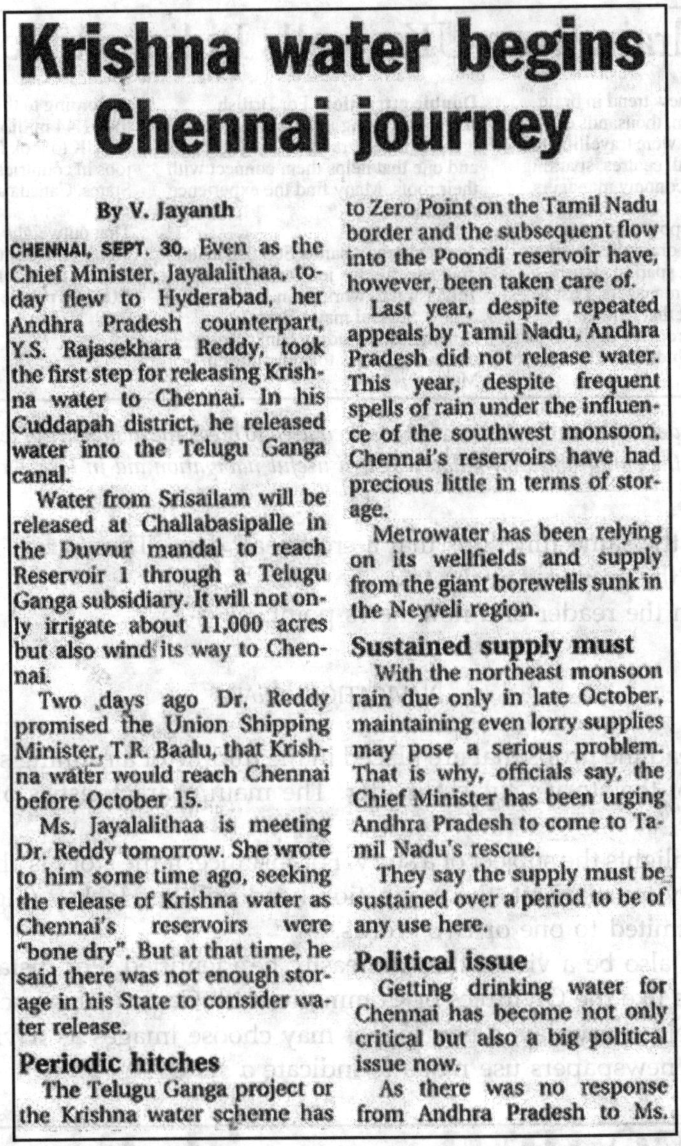

Krishna water begins Chennai journey

By V. Jayanth

CHENNAI, SEPT. 30. Even as the Chief Minister, Jayalalithaa, today flew to Hyderabad, her Andhra Pradesh counterpart, Y.S. Rajasekhara Reddy, took the first step for releasing Krishna water to Chennai. In his Cuddapah district, he released water into the Telugu Ganga canal.

Water from Srisailam will be released at Challabasipalle in the Duvvur mandal to reach Reservoir 1 through a Telugu Ganga subsidiary. It will not only irrigate about 11,000 acres but also wind its way to Chennai.

Two days ago Dr. Reddy promised the Union Shipping Minister, T.R. Baalu, that Krishna water would reach Chennai before October 15.

Ms. Jayalalithaa is meeting Dr. Reddy tomorrow. She wrote to him some time ago, seeking the release of Krishna water as Chennai's reservoirs were "bone dry". But at that time, he said there was not enough storage in his State to consider water release.

Periodic hitches

The Telugu Ganga project or the Krishna water scheme has to Zero Point on the Tamil Nadu border and the subsequent flow into the Poondi reservoir have, however, been taken care of.

Last year, despite repeated appeals by Tamil Nadu, Andhra Pradesh did not release water. This year, despite frequent spells of rain under the influence of the southwest monsoon, Chennai's reservoirs have had precious little in terms of storage.

Metrowater has been relying on its wellfields and supply from the giant borewells sunk in the Neyveli region.

Sustained supply must

With the northeast monsoon rain due only in late October, maintaining even lorry supplies may pose a serious problem. That is why, officials say, the Chief Minister has been urging Andhra Pradesh to come to Tamil Nadu's rescue.

They say the supply must be sustained over a period to be of any use here.

Political issue

Getting drinking water for Chennai has become not only critical but also a big political issue now.

As there was no response from Andhra Pradesh to Ms.

Fig. 5.8: *Crossheads used in a Krishna water story in the* Hindu.

(b) It is set in a bold typeface though its point size generally is the same as that of body text.

(c) It is used to introduce a new point in a running story.

(d) In items like city briefs or crime briefs it is used as a headline for a new item.

Brain drain from UK swells Indian call centres

LONDON: In a new trend in brain drain from Britain, thousands of British graduates were travelling to work in Indian call centres, sparking worries among economy managers.

A World Bank report stated that Britain has lost more skilled workers than any country, sparking worries among economy managers. Last week, a survey revealed that British graduates were prepared to fill as many as 16000 jobs in Indian call centres by 2009.

Double attraction: For British Asians, working in Indian call centres has a double attraction - they get a job, and one that helps them connect with their roots. Many find the experience rewarding.

A recent report said a Scottish history graduate quit his job for Sky Television to work in an Indian call centre. Several major British companies, including banks, have outsourced work to companies in Mumbai,

According to the World Bank, more than 1.44 million graduates have left the UK to look for more highly paid jobs in countries such as the United States, Canada and Australia.

That outweighs 1.26 million immigrant graduates in the UK, leaving a net "brain loss" of some 200,000 people.

Fig. 5.9: *The sidehead* 'double attraction' *has been used to break the monotony of text, and to provide a headline for the paragraph that follows. It is a useful navigation aid in long stories.*

It performs the same functions that a crosshead does. These are:

(*a*) Break the greyness of the text.

(*b*) Inform the reader of a new news point.

NAVIGATION HEADS

These are headline props that are placed in the middle of a running story to inform the reader of the story's subject matter. The main characteristics of a navigation head are:

(*a*) It highlights the subject of a story. For instance, if the story is about a running hockey tournament, the navigation head will be Hockey (Fig. 5.10).

(*b*) It is limited to one or two words.

(*c*) It can also be a visual that can easily be identified. For instance, in sports events like the Olympics or Commonwealth Games where scores of events are held every day, a newspaper may choose images as navigation heads. Some newspapers use maps to indicate a state (Fig. 5.11).

MEG 'B' draw with Excise

Times News Network

Bangalore: For the first hour or so, much of the euphoria was located off the field even as Central Excise and Madras Engineering

HOCKEY

dream start opening their account in the very first minute of the match through K.M. Somaiah. The orange-

second half, MEG brought in the equaliser when an opportunistic Charles D'Souza was bang on target. In a goalmouth melee Charles, who was stationed right opposite

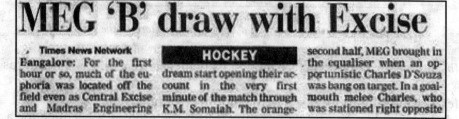

Fig. 5.10: *The navigation head* 'Hockey' *used with a running hockey tournament story.*

Governor invites party leaders for talks

By Our Special Correspondent

BANGALORE, MAY 17. Four days after the announcement of the results of the elections to the Legislative Assembly, the Governor, T.N. Chaturvedi, has initiated action for the formation of the next government in the State and end the impasse created by the fractured electoral verdict.

He has invited the State presidents of the BJP, the Congress and the Janata Dal (Secular) in the order of their strength in the new Assembly for discussions on Tuesday.

The Election Commission of India has issued the notification constituting the 12th Karnataka Legislative Assembly (since 1952).

An official press release regarding the invitation to the State unit presidents of the three parties — H.N. Ananth Kumar (BJP), B. Janardhana Poojary (Congress) and Sid-

the formation of the coalition. The Congress camp was happy that the JD(S) had reconciled itself to being part of the government and not insisting that it should support the JD(S) from outside as the Congress had been rejected by the people.

However some of the JD(S) leaders such as P.G.R. Sindhia continued to demand that the chief ministership should go to their party. Many in the JD(S) are also demanding a government on the pattern of the People's Democratic Party-Congress coalition in Jammu and Kashmir where the chief ministership is rotated between the two

For a large part of the day, Mr. Deve Gowda was closeted with his party leaders. It is learnt that being one of the leaders of the Third Front that is going to join the Congress-led government at the Centre, the JD(S) will insist on a position for Mr. Gowda befitting his standing at the national level. Mr. Gowda, who has been elected to the Lok Sabha, has been saying that he will involve himself more in national-level politics. Besides Mr. Gowda, the new Lok Sabha will have three other JD(S) members.

In the context of his name being mentioned for the chief ministership, Mr. Dharam Singh has stated that he is ready to take on any responsibility assigned to him by the party.

Mr. Singh's official residence in Kumara Park East here has become a beehive of activity.

Ever since his name began doing the

KARNATAKA

Fig. 5.11: *The map of Karnataka used as a navigation head.*

The advantages of a navigation head are:
- (*a*) It guides readers to stories of their interest.
- (*b*) It breaks greyness of text.
- (*c*) It provides a headline writer space to use more description in the main headline.

STET HEADS

These are not headline props, but headlines in their own right. However, they play the role of a headline prop because, like a navigation head, they work as beacons.

A stet head, which is also called a standing head, can be defined as a headline used for an item that is used frequently, if not every day then once a week or once a fortnight. Examples of such items are 'ET in the Classroom' (Fig. 5.12), 'World Vignettes' (5.13).

Fig. 5.12: *The stet head* 'ET in the Classroom' *used by the* Economic Times.

WORLDVIGNETTES

Fig. 5.13: *The stet head 'World Vignettes' used by the* Indian Express *on the international page.*

CHAPTER HIGHLIGHTS

Kinds of headlines props
1. Kicker or Shoulder.
2. Strapline or Reverse Shoulder.
3. Crossheads.
4. Sideheads.
5. Navigation heads.
6. Stet heads.

Characteristics of a shoulder or kicker
1. Placed on top of main headline.
2. Written in small point size.
3. Used to indicate the subject of the story.
4. Also used to indicate a news development.

Advantages of a shoulder or kicker
1. Saves space in the main headline.
2. Story subject becomes clear.

Disadvantages of a shoulder or kicker
1. It needs an extra deck.
2. Too many shoulders create a clutter.

Characteristics of strapline or reverse shoulder
1. It is run beneath the main headline.
2. It should straddle the same width as the main headline.
3. It is used as an extra hook to draw readers into a news report.
4. It is used to amplify the main news point.
5. It is used to introduce another important point.

Characteristics of a crosshead

1. Written in a point size that is generally two points more than the body type.
2. Positioned in between the running text.
3. Positioning may be flush left or centred.
4. Generally positioned after three to five paragraphs.
5. Captures the most important news point mentioned in the succeeding paragraphs.

Advantages of a crosshead

1. Breaks the greyness of text.
2. Gives readers an idea of what to expect in deep stories.

Advantages of a sidehead

1. Breaks the greyness of text.
2. Informs readers of a new news point.

Characteristics of a sidehead

1. Positioned at the start of a paragraph.
2. Set in a bold typeface, generally in body point size.
3. Used to introduce a new point in a running story.

How and when navigation heads should be used

1. Placed in the middle of a running story
2. Highlight the subject of a story.
3. Limited to one or two words.
4. Can also be a visual.

Advantages of a navigation head

1. Guides readers to stories of their interest.
2. Breaks greyness of text.
3. Releases space for the main headline.

Stet heads and their purpose

1. Headline used for an item that is used every day.
2. Work as beacons.

HEADLINE EXERCISES

Shoulder or Kicker

Exercise 1

Go through one week's newspapers and locate six headlines with a shoulder. Arrange these headlines in the following two categories:
Category 1: Headlines where the shoulder is the subject of the story.
Category 2: Headlines where the shoulder supplements the main headline by highlighting one or more than one important point in the story.

Exercise 2

Write a headline with a shoulder for each of the following three news reports using the given parameters. The shoulder can be the subject of the story or an important point that was not included in the main headline.
Main headline
Point size: 28
Case: Upper-lower
Number of letters per column: 6
Column width: 2
Number of decks: 2
Shoulder
Point size: 14
Case: Upper-lower
Number of letters per column: 14
Column width: 2
Number of decks: 1

News Report 1

NEW DELHI (UNI): Despite their increasing participation in media coverage, women journalists in the cowbelt find their job an everyday struggle, a study by the National Commission for Women has said.

"They are constantly battling discrimination at workplace in terms of salary, promotions, amenities, benefits, areas of work allotted to them and sexual harassment," the NCW's survey-status of women journalists in India says of women in the media in Madhya Pradesh, Chattisgarh, Bihar and Jharkhand.

The study conducted by the Press Institute of India (PII) says, like in the rest of the country, the number of women in the media in these states is steadily increasing, but it continues to remain a male-dominated field, one in which women have to struggle to find their own identity.

"In these four states, journalism itself has yet to establish professional norms."

In Madhya Pradesh and Chhattisgarh, the concept of women journalists with permanent jobs still does not exist, it says.

While the "lucky ones" are those on contracts with a measure of job security for two to three years, most women work without appointment letters or designations and are hired and fired on the whims of the management, the 129-page report says.

The method of payment for both men and women is not unlike that for daily wage labourers on muster rolls. They are verbally asked to begin work on a hazy work profile and at the end of the month, sign a muster roll.

"Should there be any reason for either party to terminate the 'understanding', the final settlement is made on a voucher."

Most young journalists begin their career in these states on Rs 1,500 as against starting wage of Rs 7,000 to Rs 8,000 in the Delhi newspapers.

"If a journalist has to be axed, it is most often a woman who is asked to leave."

News Report 2

KUMBAKONAM (PTI): In a grand finale to the ten-day Mahamaham festival in Kumbakonam in Tamil Nadu, about 20 lakh devotees from across the country took a holy dip and offered special pujas to invoke the blessings of Lord Shiva and Vishnu at the famous Mahamaham tank and Chakratheertham on Saturday.

The devotees who began thronging the tank since February 26, when the Mahamaham festival began, were allowed in batches of 30,000 at a time to the tank, and each batch was given five minutes to finish their pujas and take a holy bath, police said.

The two Sankaracharyas of Kanchi mutt, Jayendra Saraswathi and Vijayendra Saraswathi, the mutt heads in Madurai, Thirupanandal, Thiruvavaduthurai and Dharmapuram, and other places, were prominent among those who had the holy bath at the sprawling tank.

Billed as the Kumbha Mela of the south, the Mahamaham festival is held once in 12 years.

Earlier, all the presiding deities of the 12 Shiva temples and five Vaishnavite temples were brought to the temple tank in a procession for the 'theerthavari' (abhishek) puja during the auspicious time between 10.24 am and 12.16 pm when pandits chanted Vedic hymns.

Going by the ticket sales, an estimated 60 lakh people had visited the temple town since the festival began on February 26, a temple official said.

News Report 3

DHAKA (IANS): A UN-sponsored wildlife census has counted 668 Royal Bengal tigers in the Sundarbans—419 on the Bangladeshi side of the border and 249 on the Indian side.

The census report on the world's largest mangrove system that is the only home left for these majestic big cats released here on Saturday, also counted 21 cubs which were not added to the total count.

Among the feline denizens found in Bangladesh, 121 were male animals and the rest females.

The census funded by the United Nations Development Programme (UNDP) was conducted on the Indian side in January and on Bangladesh side Feb 26–Mar 3, Bangladesh Environment and Forests Minister Tariqul Islam said.

India's High Commissioner here Veena Sikri and UNDP resident representative Jorgen Lisner were also present at the press conference.

"The census was carried out by using the pugmark counting method that has the widest acceptability as the field staff could easily implement and which was comparatively cost-effective," the minister said.

He said tiger census would be conducted every two years.

Reverse Shoulder or Strapline

Exercise 1

Go through one week's newspapers and locate five headlines with a strapline.

Exercise 2

Write a headline with a strapline for each of the following three reports using the given parameters. Please make sure that the strapline is almost the same length as the main headline.
Main headline
Point size: 30
Case: Upper-lower
Number of letters per column: 5
Column width: 4
Number of decks: 1
Strapline
Point size: 18
Case: Upper-lower
No of letters per column: 10
Column width: 4
Number of decks: 1

News Report 1

NEW DELHI (IANS): Groundwater in Uttar Pradesh has been found to contain high doses of arsenic, known to cause cancer and several skin ailments, a leading environmental body here said Tuesday.

A survey conducted by the Centre for Science and Environment (CSE) at Ballia district in western Uttar Pradesh showed that arsenic present in the soil had contaminated the groundwater.

Attributing the problem to the increasing number of tubewells dug up in the area, Sunita Narain, CSE co-founder, said: "The problem is that we have been neglecting

---

groundwater quality so far. Even its surveillance has been totally forgotten. As a result, the water here is getting increasingly contaminated."

An analysis of water from the hand pumps in the villages and people's hair and nails has shown arsenic in alarming quantities.

The blood test performed on a village resident Ashok Singh had shown an arsenic count of 34.50 parts per billion (ppb) as against the safe level of one to four ppb.

Water from his hand pump, CSE officials said, contained 73 ppb, when the Bureau of Indian Standards maintains reference levels at 10 ppb.

According to officials here, although extensive arsenic tests by West Bengal's Jadavpur University and UNICEF had shown high contamination levels in many districts of the Gangetic plains, the government had not yet accepted it.

"The government should launch a programme to monitor the quality of groundwater and regulate the number of tubewells.

The Gangetic plains are in fact a rain-rich region. So it should be possible to use just surface water for drinking so that people escape slow death from arsenic-laden water," Narain said.

News Report 2

LUCKNOW (IANS): Seven people were killed and five seriously injured in a cracker factory blast in Uttar Pradesh, police said.

The victims included two four-year-olds and a middle-aged woman. Three of the injured were stated to be in a critical condition with 80-90 per cent burns.

The incident occurred on Thursday night in Haidergarh, a small town about 48 km from here, in the house of a man named Siraj, who was running a small licensed cracker manufacturing unit from there.

Siraj was not present when the blast occurred around 11 p.m.

"A matchstick flung after lighting a 'bidi' ignited the gunpowder stored in the house for making crackers and blew up the whole structure," a police officer said.

This was the third such incident in the past two weeks.

Three people died in a blast in a cracker unit in Mohanlalganj village, about 28 km from here, in the first week of October. One person died in a blast in Gosainganj on Wednesday.

News Report 3

NEW DELHI (PTI): The government on Thursday raised the income tax exemption limit to Rs one lakh while imposing a two per cent education cess on taxable income.

Finance Minister P Chidambaram, presenting the Union budget for 2004-05 in the Lok Sabha said the proposal to raise the IT exemption limit to Rs one lakh would give relief to 1.4 crore assessees.

Family pension received by widows, children and nominated heirs of members of the armed forces and the paramilitary forces killed in action will be exempted from income tax.

Gifts from unrelated persons above the limit of Rs. 25,000 is to be taxed as income while gifts received from blood relations, lineal ascendants and lineal descendants and gifts received on the occasion of marriage upto a limit of Rs one lakh will continue to be exempt from tax computation.

Tax on long-term capital gains from securities transactions is to be abolished and instead a tax on transactions in securities on stock exchanges is to be levied on the buyer at the rate of 0.15 per cent of the security value.

Announcing these measures, the Finance Minister said that out of nearly 3.40 crore people filing income tax returns, only 2.70 crore assessees are tax payers and the new proposals will give relief to 1.40 crore assessees.

Crosshead

Exercise 1

Go through one month's newspapers and locate three news reports that have used crossheads. Note where a crosshead has been used in the report, and the news point it highlights.

Exercise 2

Write crossheads after every three paragraphs in the following two news reports:

News Report 1

BANGALORE (ENS): Bangalore's theatre lovers formed serpentine queues and politely pushed and jostled to bag prime seats at the Chowdiah Memorial Hall last weekend, where the play Manto-Ismat Haazir Hain was staged.

The play, directed by Naseeruddin Shah, was organised by the NGO Communication for Development (CDL).

The play was a series of four short stories by celebrated Urdu writers Saadat Hasan Manto and Ismat Chughtai. Some brilliant play-acting and engaging narration enthralled the audience.

The Hindustani that the actors spoke might have come across as a little tough at times, but any such communication gap was filled by the excellent performances of the actors.

The narrator had an innovative way of getting the audience to switch off cell phones — he pulled out his own ringing phone from his pocket and turned it off. But in spite of this example, the irritating instruments kept crying out through the performance.

The first half saw Manto's two stories, *Bu* and *Titwal Ka Kutta*. The first was the only one that did not quite match up to the rest in theme. The one-man act of Bu was both narration and play-acting. The invisible characters also took life with the actor's words and emotions.

This was the story of a young man and his heady sexual encounter with a young 'ghati' woman on a rainy day, and the intoxicating smell of her body.

Titwal Ka Kutta is a satire that had much relevance on Monday too, though it was written in the last century. A scathing dig on Indo-Pak relations, it talks of a dog caught between troops of the two countries on a check-post in the mountains. Jamil Khan did a wonderful job in juggling the roles of the Indian soldiers and their Pakistani counterparts.

Post-interval, it was Ismat's turn. *Lihaaf*, the story that brought Ismat both fame and trouble for having tackled homosexuality, was wonderfully performed by Heeba Shah. Through the eyes of a young girl, the world of adults seems both funny and scary at the same time.

The last was *Un Byaahaton Ke Naam*, an account of Manto's and Ismat's court trial on charges of obscenity in their writings. This was also the only one among the four stories that had more than one actor on stage. The humour and sarcasm that held its sway through the story gave in to nostalgia and a little sorrow as the play concluded with a group song of sorts.

The play was organised by CDL as part of its 'Theatre That Matters' series. In the last three years, they have brought plays like *Mahatma Vs Gandhi*, *Women Can't Wait* and *Tumhari Amrita* as part of the series.

News Report 2

HYDERABAD (ENS): The stage is set for the first direct talks between PWG leaders and the Andhra Pradesh government here on Friday though opinion is divided on how successful they will be.

The two groups, the People's War Group (PWG) and the Communist Party of India-Marxist Leninist (CPI-ML) Janashakti, would hold talks over three to four days with an eight-member state government team in the presence of eight mediators comprising civil liberties activists and journalists.

But a meeting ground might be elusive.

The Naxals have already made it clear that the talks were aimed only at "exposing the government's sincerity towards addressing the real issues of people".

However, the government sees the talks as an opportunity to end the protracted problem and usher in lasting peace.

"If you don't avail of this opportunity it might not come again for a long time," Chief Minister Y.S. Rajasekhara Reddy told PWG leaders.

The Chief Minister held a meeting with his officials to fine tune the government's strategy. He asked them to showcase the efforts made by the government during the last six months to uplift the poor and weaker sections of society.

Land distribution among tillers and the poor and an end to World Bank dictated economic policies are two important issues in the 11-point agenda for the talks mooted by the Maoists.

Sources in the government said while it was willing to "go the extra mile" to address issues raised by the rebels, it would also make it clear that it would not be possible to meet demands which were outside the nation's constitutional and legal framework.

The government, for instance, may not agree to Maoist leaders carrying weapons during the talks. It would also express its helplessness on issues like putting an end to policies of globalisation and granting statehood to the Telangana region.

Leading the Maoist guerrilla groups in the talks would be PWG's Ramakrishna, who surfaced in public on Monday after two decades of being underground.

Andhra-Orissa Border Committee secretary Sudhakar alias Balakrishna and North Telangana Special Zone committee member G. Ravi alias Ganesh would also participate.

Janashakti would be represented by its leaders Amar and Riyaz. Protected by extraordinary security, the leaders have been in Hyderabad for the last three days.

The government team would be represented by state Home Minister K. Jana Reddy as well as three other state ministers and Congress leaders.

Maoist violence has taken the lives of nearly 6,000 people in the state during the last 35 years.

Sidehead

Exercise 1

Go through one month's newspapers and locate three news reports that have used sideheads. Note where a sidehead has been used in the report, and the point it highlights.

Exercise 2

Write sideheads after every two paragraphs in the following two reports:

News Report 1

JAIPUR (UNI): More than 19,000 tribals in eight Rajasthan districts are on the verge of becoming homeless because of official orders relating to forest land, activists fighting for their rights said today.

Applications relating to nearly 19,000 claims had been filed by tribals in the districts, yet no government committee has made site visits so far for their settlement, Ramesh Nandwana, convenor of the 'Jungel Jameen Jan Andolan', said.

A delegation of tribals and activists met Chief Minister Vasundhara Raje today seeking her intervention into the matter. They would be meeting state Forests Minister Laxminarayan Dave later in the day.

The activists claimed that the tribals had been staying on the forest land for more than 30 years, yet were being asked to vacate the area now. "They own 5-6 bighas of land, which is all they have," Mr Nandwana said.

Most of the tribals being evicted are Bhils and Garasias who have taken to agriculture on lands where they have lived for centuries, he argued.

The tribals would be forced to launch agitations if their claims are not settled at the earliest, he said.

Tribals from Pali, Udaipur, Sirohi, Dungarpur, Banswara, Baran, Chittorgarh and Rajasmand are among those who have received eviction notices from the forest department, he said.

News Report 2

CHENNAI (IANS): A rare large whale shark which got entangled in fishing nets, off the Chennai coast, was brought ashore by fishermen but died on the way to a quiet beach south of this Tamil Nadu capital.

The whale shark is a protected species, rarely sighted in the Bay of Bengal, Chennai's wildlife warden K.S.S.V.P. Reddy said on Friday.

Scientists from the Zoological Survey of India, the Central Marine Fisheries Research Institute and the National Biodiversity Authority rushed to the beach on Thursday to save the male whale shark, which was 4.5 m long and weighed nearly two tonnes. But they were too late.

Fishermen had tried to drag the black shark with white spots to shore but it died in the process. They were then busy attempting to cut it in pieces for its meat and fins, which fetch a good price in the market.

They were stopped by authorities who dug a 10-ft deep pit in the beach and buried the creature of the deep with the help of a crane. A guard was posted to ensure it was not dug up later.

Marine experts mourned the fact that the shark, which was brought under Schedule 1 of the Wildlife Protection Act in 1972, was killed by the fishermen.

National Biodiversity Authority secretary K. Venkataraman, who also visited the beach, said it was difficult for the authorities to convince the fishermen that they were prohibited from bringing in catch like this.

"I have for long wished to see a whale shark. I have never been able to sight one even in the waters around the Andaman Islands where they are supposed to be found. To find such a specimen off Chennai's coast shows these creatures still live in these waters," he said.

This species of the whale shark are not hunters and killers but feed on planktons.

Navigation Head

Exercise 1

Go through important newspapers of the city and collect the different styles in which navigation heads are used. Discuss their advantages and disadvantages with your instructor.

6

FEATURE AND MAGAZINE HEADLINES

FEATURE HEADLINES

The five most popular writing formats used in a newspaper are: inverted pyramid; question-answer; and narrative, descriptive or analytical. The inverted pyramid format is used to write hard news stories. These reports present facts as they are; there is no comment, no analysis and no speculation. The headlines for these news reports are therefore stark and functional. They are built around nouns and verbs and highlight the most important point in a story.

The question-answer format is used sparingly, is generally limited to short interviews and is used to supplement the main story. Full-length interviews are used when the subjects are very important and happen to be the leaders of countries or celebrities. Otherwise, the interviews are paraphrased and news reports built from the important points made in the interview. The headlines are picked up from the most controversial or provocative point made by the subject. They are then used as direct quotes (see Chapter 4).

The headlines where the most creativity is required are the ones that are written for narrative, descriptive or analytical stories, also known as features stories. These reports use a variety of writing styles and may focus on a single, dominant point or a multiplicity of points. They also cover a wide range of subjects and can be classified as news, political, business, entertainment, human interest, sports, development features, etc.

There was a time when analytical or political reports were not included in this category. Instead, the features were limited to light, offbeat stories largely pertaining to women, children, health, education, development, etc. These stories were broadly referred to as soft stories, feature stories or human interest reports and were meant to add variety to a newspaper whose primary job was to provide news.

Today, the traditional newspaper has undergone a major metamorphosis. The change has been caused by three factors: the challenge posed by television, the arrival of new technology and the changing aspirations of readers. Newspapers no longer limit themselves to hard news reports alone, but provide news behind the news, analyse the implications of news developments, mirror the social and business trends in the society and economy and provide information on all issues that touch the lives of a reader, even if they happen to be as mundane as gardening or as hi-tech as rocket science or as bewildering as finance.

The newspapers also present these reports differently so that they are not confused with hard news stories, which is pure reportage. In the past these reports would have been found only on the pages of the Sunday pull-out, also called the Sunday Magazine. Today, however, almost all mainstream Indian newspapers bring out weekly or fortnightly supplements which deal with subjects like fashion, entertainment, arts, science, information technology, health, women, law, media, development, etc.

Several newspapers have launched city pull-outs to cover the city happenings in a narrative or a descriptive format, and more newspapers are adding OpEd pages (pages facing the Editorial page) to display in depth political, social and economic features. The trend is not limited to mainstream newspapers. Business newspapers too have gone beyond news reports and launched a range of supplements that provide information in user-friendly formats on issues like money and finance, investments, mutual funds, the corporate world, new products, market trends, etc.

This has not only changed the way in which feature stories are written, but also the way in which feature headlines are written and displayed. Two styles are used by newspapers to display features.

Traditional Format

This style is used to display news features — that is features written to supplement breaking news. These features are run on the news pages and assist the reader by providing lucid interpretations, background information or stories related to news developments. An important purpose of these features is to bring out the human element behind the breaking news, and add variety and depth to news coverage

The news features use a narrative, descriptive or analytical style of writing and are displayed like news reports. The headlines for these features are generally creative and are written in the standard news format. The most that a headline writer does is to use a light typeface or italics to make the headline look visually different. Interestingly, there is no special typographical treatment for news features. If the newspaper style permits, the headline writer may use kickers or straplines to add meaning to the feature headline.

For instance, when Mr Prakash Karat became the General Secretary of the Communist Party of India (Marxist) and his wife, Mrs Brinda Karat, became a member of the CPI (M) politbureau, the *Hindustan Times* came up with a brilliant headline (Fig. 6.1). The headline used a shoulder to indicate that the story was a news feature — a profile — and not a hard news story.

Fig. 6.1: *A headline written for a news feature that was displayed on the front page of the* Hindustan Times. *The headline is written in the same format that is used for news headlines.*

A similar creative headline was written for another news feature in the newspaper. This news feature was a curtain raiser that was run on the arrival of Chinese Premier Wen Jiabao to India (Fig. 6.2). The headline punned on the title of the popular film *Crouching Tiger, Hidden Dragon,* but used the typeface and type style in which news headlines are written.

Fig. 6.2: *A feature headline written for a curtain raiser that was used on the eve of the arrival of the Chinese Premier to India.*

Another good headline for a news feature was the one that was written for a news analysis on the woes of RSS bodies, popularly known as the Sangh Parivar (Fig. 6.3). The analysis appeared on the news pages and used the typical news format.

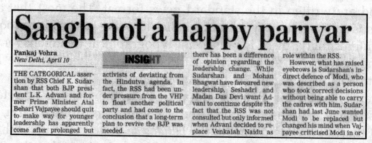

Fig. 6.3: *A headline written for a news analysis in the* Hindustan Times. *The headline plays on the words 'Sangh Parivar', which was the subject of the story.*

Similarly, when Prince Charles got married to Ms Camilla Parker Bowles, Reuters moved a news feature focusing on royal marriages. The feature gave details of the marriages of Queen Elizabeth's four children and the fact that three of the marriages ended in a divorce. It was a very readable news feature. Unfortunately, the headline used was a label headline.

Original headline
Royal marriages: The success and failure stories
Revised headline
4 marriages, 3 divorces; no marital bliss for UK's royals

Display Format

The display format is used for features run on special pages or supplements. The headlines for these features are mostly written in a large point size, and often in a special typeface. They use a fewer number of words and depend on supporting straplines, shoulders, blurbs, photographs or graphics to communicate the message. This often reduces the feature headline to a minor element in a larger scheme of affairs.

However, this does not mean that these headlines are overshadowed by design. On the contrary, more thought goes into writing these headlines because the writers have very little space to write a meaningful headline. This is one reason why headline writers rely on puns, similes, alliterations or on clever turns of phrase to write these headlines.

Four different kinds of formats are used to write these feature headlines. These formats, incidentally, are decided by the design editor or the visualizer, who decides the:
1. Point size, font style and colour to be used in writing the headline.
2. Photographs, illustrations or graphics that will be used to support the headline.
3. Point size, font style and colour to write the strapline/blurb.
4. Placement of these three elements on the page.
The four formats used to display headlines for features are:

Use of Varying Typefaces

In this case the colour and size of the font is used to make the headline look different to other headlines on the page.

A good headline where typographic contrast was used to deliver the message was the one that was used for a story on Value Added Tax (VAT). The feature was written to inform the readers about VAT and dispel the misgivings created in the minds of the common man by the traders who went on a three-day strike before its implementation. The headline was simple but its impact was great, thanks to the use of words in bold and light shades of black (Fig. 6.4). The main headline was supported by a strapline, written in reverse.

The stage is set for implementation of Value Added Tax from April 1. Do we need to worry?

Fig. 6.4: *A headline used in the* New Indian Express on Sunday. *The headline uses typography to enhance the visual impact.*

Use of Photographs as Props

In this format, the headline derives meaning from the photograph. The headline may be superimposed on the photograph or placed next to the photograph. Sometimes, a blurb or strapline may be used to convey extra meaning.

The headline written on the vanishing tigers in Sariska in the *New Indian Express on Sunday* is a good example of this style of headline writing. The headline was made of a single word with an exclamation mark:

Maneaten!

The headline would have conveyed no meaning if it was not propped by the photograph of a morose looking tiger. One look at the headline and the photograph was enough to understand what the headline writer sought to convey—it was man who had eaten the tigers (Fig. 6.5).

With no tigers being found in the sanctuary, what goes on is a blame-game between the officials and the villagers and a science that is inept to count the tigers

Fig. 6.5: *A headline used in the* New Indian Express on Sunday. *The headline uses the photograph of a tiger to convey meaning.*

Another outstanding feature headline in the same format was written on a health column that spoke about the faltering sexual drives of men between the ages of 40 and 55. This headline was not only superimposed on the photograph, but was both provocative and meaningful.

MEN too must PAUSE

The design editor added value to the headline by placing it over a thought provoking photograph. Use of contrasting typefaces and the strapline reinforced the message further (Fig. 6.6).

Fig. 6.6: *A headline used in the* New Indian Express *on Sunday. The headline uses a play on words to communicate meaning; contrasting types, a photograph and a strapline are used to add meaning to the headline.*

Use of Illustrations as Props

Design editors sometimes use illustrations to prop news features, especially those that are written for the Op Ed pages or for the Sunday edition. This is done to add variety to the page. A good example of such a headline was the one that was written on the dilemma of the Manmohan Singh government on the issue of FDI in the *Economic Times*. The headline used the proverb 'caught in a cleft stick' intelligently to indicate that Dr Singh's dilemma had something to do with the Left parties.

Caught in a (c)left stick

However, it was the illustration that showed Dr Manmohan Singh trying to avoid a sickle shaped swing that gave the relevant context to the headline and made it complete (Fig. 6.7).

Fig. 6.7: *An illustration used to add meaning to a headline in the* Economic Times.

Use of Graphics as Props

Feature headlines play a similar subordinate role in graphics. A good example is the analytical story on the sons of film stars who have not been able to capitalize on the name of their illustrious parents, and play second fiddle to Bollywood's superstar Shahrukh Khan. The headline was a clever pun but it needed a strapline to understand what the story's thrust was. The display once again was terrific (Fig. 6.8).

Main headline: **It's in the son sign**
Strapline: **No matter how they try, star sons can't shake off SRK**

TEN TIPS TO WRITE A FEATURE HEADLINE

All feature headlines must be creative, irrespective of whether they are written with or without visual or typographical props. Here are 10 tips to write a feature headline.

Tip 1: Play on Words

To write these headlines, the headline writers first need to identify the theme of the story. For instance, a body building feature published in the *Telegraph*, a

Fig. 6.8: *A feature headline in the* Economic Times *that is part of a graphic.*

newspaper that takes great pride in its creative headlines, talked about how a school for body builders had made life miserable for residents and passers by. The body builders, according to the report, passed lewd comments on young women who passed by the school. The headline writer punned on the word body to come up with a gem of a headline. In just two words, the headline writer had captured both the subject and the theme of the story:

Bawdy builders

Another great headline from the same newspaper was used for a sports page feature that talked about the running of a stable. The writer spoke at length about the scrubbing of horses, their food habits, their daily exercise, their intensive grooming, etc. It was a highly informative and educative feature on horses and the headline writer did justice to the feature writer's skills by coming up with the following headline:

Stable manners

Similarly, some of the headlines that were written on the United Front government headed by Mr H.D. Deve Gowda during the 1990s were absolutely arresting. That was the first coalition government formed at the centre by a grouping of 13 parties, and there were always fears that the coalition would fall apart. The front was called a disunited front because it was made of 13 parties with differing ideologies and policies; its stress on caste came in for particular ridicule, as also the fact that it had members whom nobody had heard of. Here is a selection of some of the headlines written for the Op Ed page features on the Deve Gowda government:

Disunited Front
National Affront
Caste no bar
Backward Front
House of common's

Tip 2: Play on Names of Individuals

The names of several celebrities lend themselves beautifully to the writing of creative headlines, especially when it comes to profiles. For instance, when the legendary British umpire Dickie Bird retired, the headline writer used his surname to headline the profile written on the occasion.

Free as a Bird

A similar brilliant headline was written about the Shiv Sena leader, Mr Bal Thackeray, when he was summoned to the court in an election case. The report was an informative backgrounder that was done by the newspaper and sought to enlighten the reader on the pros and cons of the case.

Bal in nation's court

Tip 3: Play on Acronyms

Business newspapers revel in using acronyms. This happens because most financial organizations or financial terms are long and unwieldy. The only way to fit them in headlines is to reduce them to acronyms. This headline characteristic spills into writing headlines for business features too.

The business newspapers were particularly delighted when Mr P Chidambaram became the Finance Minister in the UPA government in 2004. Since PC is the acronym for personal computers most headline writers used computer terminology to describe the Finance Minister's activities, especially in business features that reviewed or commented on the actions of the Finance Minister.

A headline that stood out was the one that was written on an analytical feature on the Finance Minister's meeting with the captains of Indian industry soon after taking charge in 2004. The headline did not give any information as to what can be expected from the meeting between the Finance Minister and top Indian industrialists. Yet, it caught the eye because of the play on words.

PC logs on to India Inc

Another headline that caught the eye was the one that related to Mr Chidambaram's use of the Internet to locate personal staff. The report was written as a news feature and needed a slightly different headline.

PC hits net for personal staff

Interestingly, computer terminology was not used as puns or active verbs when writing headlines for stories related to Mr P. Chidambaram when he was a Union Minister in the 1990s. The reason for that was simple: the computers or the Internet had not taken off in India then. The rule that flows from this example is that only those puns should be used in feature, and news, headlines that can be easily understood by the common reader.

The puns are not limited to the names of individuals on business pages. Treaties and financial terms are also punned frequently to add life to business features. GATT, the acronym for General Agreement on Tariffs and Trade, has produced a wide range of witty headlines because its acronym sounds almost like *got*.

Give it all you've GATT

Tip 4: Play on Titles of Books

Well known book titles are used as feature headlines whenever they fit the story theme. The novel *A Tale of Two Cities* by Charles Dickens has been used on numerous occasions as a headline for a story that concerns two cities, two individuals, two countries, two rivers, etc.

The *New Indian Express* used a variation of the title to headline an analytical feature on two leading south Indian politicians—K. Karunakaran of Kerala and M. Karunanidhi of Tamil Nadu (Fig. 6.9)

Book titles have been used not only as feature headlines but also as headlines for editorials.

War and Peace
Mother India
On razor's edge
Flight into danger
A Himalayan Blunder

How two men, both in their eighties, dominated politics in South India in 2004

Fig. 6.9: *A feature headline written in the* New Indian Express *on Sunday that plays on the title of the book* A Tale of Two Cities.

Headline writers must avoid overuse of the same titles as this turns them into clichés. A good policy should be to play on words instead of using the title in its original format. This will impart the headline freshness every time the book title is used.

Tip 5: Play on Film Titles

Popular film titles also make great headlines. One film whose title has been used repeatedly in recent years is *Crouching Tiger, Hidden Dragon*. It was used to headline a curtain raiser—which was a news feature—written on the eve of the Chinese Premier's visit to India (Fig. 6.2). A cover story in the magazine section of the *New Indian Express* played upon the same title to write a headline for a story on the abuse of women in the film industry (Fig. 6.10). This shows how varied is the use of film titles—they can be used to fit several different themes and moods.

Casting couch in the film industry makes interesting gossip, but in the real world, thousands of women employees cope up with sexual harassment silently

Fig. 6.10: *A play on the title of the film* Crouching Tiger, Hidden Dragon.

The *Times of India* played on the film title *King Kong* and wrote this marvellous headline when Ms Sonia Gandhi helped the Congress win power in 2004.

Queen Cong

Tip 6: Play on Radio and Television Jingles

Catchy punchlines used in print advertisement or radio and television jingles are increasingly being used as a source of creative headlines. Like book titles, jingles have a high recall and can generate both humour and creativity.

A good example is Onida's commercial whose slogan *Neighbour's envy, India's pride* was recast to generate this headline on India's cricket captain Saurav Ganguly who comes from the state of West Bengal:

Saurav is Bengal's joy, India's pride

Tip 7: Play on Phonetics

A play on spellings of words produces good headlines. The *Times of India* came up with a great headline when India's hockey star Dhanraj Pillay was dropped from the hockey team in 2004. Officially, Pillay had been rested. However, there were few takers for this argument advanced by the Indian Hockey Federation (IHF) headed by another celebrity K.P.S. Gill. The headline writer modified the IHF chief's name Gill into Gill-ty to great effect.

Pillay supporters hold IHF Gill-ty

The news feature analysing the impact of Uma Bharati's announcement that she is taking *sanyas* from politics generated another creative headline. 'TraUma' was the word chosen by the headline writer; it expressed the anguish within the party at the *sanyasin's* announcement. The name Uma which formed part of the word 'Trauma' was placed in screen for the reader to understand the reason for the trauma (Fig. 6.11).

Fig. 6.11: *Good use of phonetics in a headline on Uma Bharati written in the* Indian Express.

Another headline where phonetics produced an equally powerful impact was the one written for a feature on perfumes in the *Asian Age* (Fig. 6.12). The headline writer coined the word 'Scenterstage' to stress the central place that perfumes are now occupying in the common Indian's life.

Fig. 6.12: *An imaginative headline generated by coining a word around scents, which was the story's main theme in the Sunday issue of the* Asian Age.

Headlines based on phonetics are not always produced by addition of alphabets. Sometimes, changing the meaning of a word through innovative usage produces gems. An outstanding example of this genre is the headline written for the comprehensive defeat of Mr Chandrababu Naidu's Telugu Desam party in the 2004 Assembly elections. The writer brought out the enormity of the defeat by this usage:

Land slides under Babu

Tip 8: Play on Proverbs and Sayings

Like book and film titles, proverbs and sayings are also another resource for a creative editor to tap. They enjoy a high recall value and help separate feature headlines from news headlines. Their value increases further when headline writers use variants of well known sayings to make their point.

When Dr Manmohan Singh addressed his first press conference after becoming the Prime Minister the know-all Delhi newsmen thought that the economist-turned politician would be easy meat for their barbs. One headline writer even captured this mood (Fig. 6.13) and turned around the proverb cat among the pigeons to say:

A pigeon among the cats

It is another matter that Dr Singh put up a polished performance, leaving the newsmen gasping.

The phrase 'winds of change' was modified to write a catchy headline for a Tamil Nadu story that spoke about the change that was brought in the lives of rural

151

Feature and Magazine Headlines

Fig. 6.13: *A good turn of the proverb cat among the pigeons in the* Hindu.

women following the setting up of a marketing company by a non-governmental organization (NGO). The company paid good money to these women who went deep into the forests to gather plants that had medicinal value. The feature headline was backed by a photograph and a strapline to produce extra effect (Fig. 6.14).

Fig. 6.14: *An imaginative headline written in the* New Indian Express on Sunday *based on a play on the phrase* winds of change.

The *Asian Age* produced a similar twist when it headlined the story of Veerappan's killing in a police encounter. The headline writer turned around the vengeful saying 'an eye for an eye' for the following headline:

An eye for many eyes

There could not have been a more apt headline for Veerappan who was said to have killed 150 people and 2,000 elephants in his two-decade long reign of terror. Mysteriously, Veerappan's body that was brought for the post mortem examination after the encounter that led to his death had only one eye.

Tip 9: Play on Themes/Images

Sometimes politicians get identified with pet themes or images. Mr Clean was the epithet applied to the late Rajiv Gandhi before Bofors caught up with him. In the case of former Andhra Pradesh Chief Minister, Mr Chandrababu Naidu, everything came to be related to computers and the Internet. The capital of Andhra Pradesh came to be referred to as Cyberabad and the state itself as Cyber Pradesh.

It was not a surprise that headline writers rushed to pun on his cyber image when he lost power in 2004. Some of the headlines that were written to mark the event were:

Chandrababu exits, Congress to reboot
Cong storms Naidu's cyberland
System failure: Cyber CM logged out

The imagery did not stop with cyber verbs and nouns. It also extended to the election symbol of Mr Naidu, which was a bicycle.

Andhra Pradesh voters puncture the bicycle

Tip 10: Creative Use of Verbs

Verbs add sparkle to headlines when they are derived from the subject of a story and are used in the active voice. India's wicket keeper Parthiv Patel had a harrowing time when a fake marriage was registered in his name in Rajkot. The headline writer used two cricketing terms 'bouncer' and 'stumps' to write an imaginative headline (Fig. 6.15).

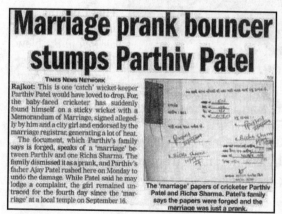

Fig. 6.15: *Imaginative use of the verb stumps and bouncer in a Parthiv Patel headline in the* Times of India.

In fact, sports desks have been the most imaginative in the use of verbs. They have converted several nouns into powerful action verbs.

Bubka vaults **to new life**
Carl Lewis sprints **into history books**
Anju makes the leap **of her life**
Rathore shoots **a silver lining on a cloudy day**
Russians basket **second string Americans**

Magazine Headlines

Magazine headlines have traditionally been different from newspaper headlines. This is because magazines do not use the inverted pyramid style of reporting as newspapers do. Their writing is more free flowing and is based on trends, reviews, analysis and interpretation of events. The magazine headlines therefore need to reflect the theme of the article, instead of being restricted to one key or dominant point.

Magazines also run one article to a page or few pages. This allows them to treat their headlines differently. The headlines are shorter, mostly limited to two to three words only—a restriction that requires greater imagination and creativity on the part of the headline writer. The result has been the evolution of figurative headlines—headlines that pun or play upon words to convey meaning.

The trend has continued to this day, though newspapers have started moving closer to magazine headlines in their lifestyle or feature sections. However, magazines have tried to maintain their distinct identity both in writing and design. News magazines, in particular, have evolved their own distinct style of headline writing which is more uniform and consistent than the lifestyle magazines devoted to fashion, films, racing, etc.

The following are the broad rules used by the magazines to write headlines:

Format

Most magazines prefer a three-level format, though strictly speaking the first level cannot be considered a part of the headline. For instance, *India Today* (Fig. 6.16), in its 2004 issues used the first level to denote the page head or the department head. The page head also works as a shoulder or a kicker. If it is a state report, the kicker lists the name of the state; if it is an international report, the kicker lists the name of the country; if it is a back of the book story, the kicker mentions whether the story is about food or fashion.

The second level is the main headline. It is written in a large typeface. The positioning of this headline need not be on top of the story. Depending on the design needs, the main headline may be positioned in the middle of a story, flush left, flush

Fig. 6.16: *The format adopted by* India Today *to write headlines.*

right or even superimposed on a photograph. The main headline invariably is a play on words, and is limited to two to three words, rarely more.

The third level is made of a strapline. This is an extra hook used by the headline writer to explain the main point of the story. Stripped of the design attributes, the three-tier headline would read as:

Shoulder/Kicker:	**States Andhra Pradesh**
Main headline:	**ROLL OF DISHONOUR**
Strapline:	**Two recipients of the 2003 President's Police Medal for Gallantry now face an inquiry for getting the award fraudulently. This reveals only the tip of the iceberg.**

A similar format is adopted by *Outlook* though with minor variations. The magazine does not carry the department head on top of the page; instead this is listed in small points at the base of the page. The page head, if it can be so called, is the shoulder or flag that lists the subject of the story. The main headline is run in a large typeface beneath the shoulder. Once again the positioning of this headline varies. It can be on top of the page, flush left, flush right or in the middle of the page. In this example (Fig. 6.17), the main headline is run in the lower half of the page below a photograph.

Fig. 6.17: *The format adopted by* Outlook *to write headlines.*

The strapline in a smaller typeface makes up the third part. The full headline in this example reads as follows:

Shoulder/Kicker:	**WEAVERS**
Main headline:	**Looms of Doom**
Strapline:	**A foreign fabric has silenced the looms of the local weavers, reduced them to poverty and killed an art.**

It is interesting to note that both the magazines use different fonts and typestyles for each element of the headline—shoulder, main headline and strapline. Quite clearly, both these news magazines look at headlines as important design tools. From time to time, they change their headline typestyles, positioning and even the format.

Other magazines too attach equal importance to the headline format. The *Week* (Fig. 6.18) too prefers a three-tier format with the subject line going as the shoulder. This is followed by the main headline which is a play on words and the strapline.

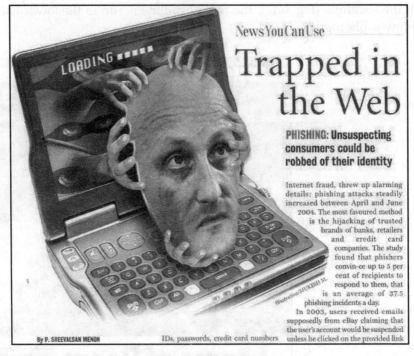

Fig. 6.18: *The headline format adopted by the* Week.

Figurative Usage

The second key characteristic of a magazine headline is the pun on words or use of alliterations, similes, etc., in the main headline. The *Outlook* injected new life into the Shakespearean phrase 'To be or not to be' in a story pertaining to engineering colleges in Punjab and Haryana (Fig. 6.19).

Fig. 6.19: *An eye-catching headline in* Outlook.

Another book title that was used cleverly by the same magazine pertained to a column written by cricketer Greg Chappell outlining the favourable swing in the fortunes of English cricket in August 2004 (Fig. 6.20). The headline punned on the fact that the month of August belonged to the English cricketers, which incidentally was also the title of a well known book written by an Indian, Upamanyu Chatterjee.

Fig. 6.20: *The book title* An English August *used imaginatively in* Outlook.

The story exposing the fraudulent sale of grains meant for economically weaker groups by Indian exporters used a headline 'The Grain Drain' — a clever pun on the phrase 'brain drain' (Fig. 6.21).

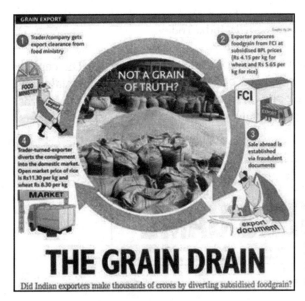

Fig. 6.21: *A very appropriate pun on the phrase 'brain drain' used in* Outlook.

India Today, which has come to be known for alliterations that it uses in headlines, used a good one while talking of the Congress party's social programme (Fig. 6.22).

Fig. 6.22: *An example of alliteration used by* India Today.

The magazine also used a good pun on the story on religious census. The census figures that were released in 2004, instead of being looked upon as valuable statistics, became the centre of a huge political row with each party using the figures for its own benefit. The magazine appropriately headlined the story as 'Numbers Game' (Fig. 6.23).

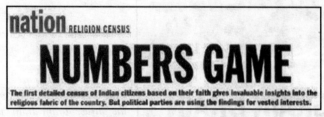

Fig. 6.23: *A good pun on the politics of appropriating the census figures on religion.*

Description

The magazines realize that it is not enough to have a clever headline; it is important to highlight the most controversial or significant point in the story. The strapline, placed strategically beneath the main headline, plays this role. The strapline is not written like the standard headline. Instead it is a full sentence, sometimes two sentences, that may highlight one or more than one point, including comments and questions.

The following strapline was used by the *Outlook* magazine for the Nagpur story that detailed the lynching of a criminal in a courtroom by a mob that included scores of women:

Crime or punishment? Freedom certainly, for these women who, in a unique retribution, ended a tyrant's 14-year reign of terror

The *Week* in its cover story on medical tourism used a strapline to explain the thrust of the report (Fig. 6.24).

The country becomes a medical destination as even patients in the west fly in for world class treatment that is cheaper.

Fig. 6.24: *The strapline is an effective way to provide description in a magazine headline.*

Design Tool

After photographs and graphics, headlines are the most dominant design element on a magazine page. That is why magazines go to great lengths in deciding the positioning and display of headlines.

The news section uses headlines set in bold fonts. The Back of the Book section that features lifestyle, fashion, food or other trend stories uses simple and more elegant fonts. Similarly, special focus magazines such as those relating to cinema, cars, etc., use fonts that best express the tastes of their target audience.

Great care is taken in choosing the headline colour. Design editors insist that the headline colour must match the mood of the story. Often, the headlines are set in reverse or in screen to add contrast to the page. They are also superimposed on photographs or bled across two pages to produce greater visual impact.

Give Identity

Consistency in the writing and display of headlines plays a major role in giving a distinct identity to a magazine. A reader's eyes and mind gets attuned to the headline style adopted by a publication. The magazines too realize this. They do not change the headline fonts or display styles too often for fear of disorienting the reader.

CHAPTER HIGHLIGHTS

Kinds of feature headlines

1. Traditional.
2. Display.

Important points about display feature headlines

1. Depend on visual props that may be photographs, graphics or illustrations.

2. Design team is actively involved in planning.

3. Number of words used are few.

4. Written for features run on non-news pages.

5. Can use varied type faces and point sizes.

Characteristics of traditional feature headlines

1. Written in a news format.
2. Can use italics/light typeface at times.
3. Can be supported by shoulders/straplines.
4. Do not use visual props.
5. Do not use typographical props.
6. Design team is not involved in their writing.

Tips to write feature headlines

1. Play on words.
2. Play on names of individuals.
3. Play on acronyms.
4. Play on titles of books.
5. Play on film titles.
6. Play on radio and television jingles.
7. Play on phonetics.
8. Play on proverbs and sayings.
9. Play on themes/images.
10. Creative use of verbs.

Characteristics of magazine headlines

1. Generally, magazines use a three-tier format.
2. The first tier is made of the subject.
3. The second tier is the main headline, which is invariably a play on words.
4. The third tier sums up the main point in the story.

Positioning of magazine headlines

1. Top of the page.
2. Middle of the page.
3. Flush left/right.
4. Superimposed on a photograph.
5. Run across two pages.

Use of fonts and typestyles

1. Magazines prefer serif fonts for the main headline and non-serif fonts for the strap line.
2. The typeface should be visible when headlines are superimposed on photographs.
3. The colour is selected as per the mood of the story.
4. There should be consistency in display.
5. The fonts should not be changed too often.

HEADLINE EXERCISES

Feature Headlines

Exercise 1

Go through last month's newspapers and locate one feature headline for each of the following categories:

1. Play on names of individuals.
2. Play on acronyms.
3. Play on names with dual meanings.
4. Play on titles of books.
5. Play on film titles.

6. Play on radio and television jingles.
7. Play on phonetics.
8. Play on proverbs and sayings.
9. Play on themes/images.
10. Creative use of verbs.

Exercise 2

Write one headline for each of the following five features. The headline should not be a simple, straightforward headline but should be a play on words. There are no headline parameters. You can use your imagination to select the column widths and font sizes. Or else you can ask your instructor to lay down the parameters.

Feature 1

KHANDWA (Madhya Pradesh) (IANS): It has been 13 years since he passed away, but while Kishore Kumar lives on in his many songs and has millions of admirers, the Madhya Pradesh government is unable to maintain or restore a simple memorial in his hometown Khandwa.

One of India's most celebrated singers, Kishore Kumar still rules the airwaves with his vibrant voice and spawns a dozen imitators every day. In contrast, the memorial marking the spot where he was cremated in Khandwa is overgrown with weeds and decaying.

In the 13 years since October 13, 1987, when the legendary singer and filmmaker died in Mumbai and was cremated in Khandwa, his memorial built by the local civic authorities has literally fallen apart.

Wild grass and shrubs have grown through cracks in the memorial and several of its tiles have chipped off.

And this is despite the efforts of the people of Khandwa, who collected Rs.100,000 by contributing a rupee each in an effort coordinated by Bollywood poet-lyricist Vitthal Bhai Patel.

Patel's efforts have earned the wrath of Khandwa Mayor Tarachand Agarwal of the Bharatiya Janata Party (BJP).

"What Patel is doing is an insult to Khandwa and its people. Can't we restore the memorial?" asked Agarwal indignantly.

Undeterred, Patel said he would start the renovation within a month. The people of the area were with him, he asserted.

"The municipal corporation was in slumber all these years. And when some person has taken up the task, it is creating hurdles. We will see that Patel is able to complete the task," said Manish Jain, a resident of Khandwa.

Kishore Kumar's mellifluous voice has weathered the storms of time better than his memorial.

Maybe, in the years to come his many admirers will finally have a proper place to pay homage to him—much like Elvis fans in Memphis or Jim Morrison devotees in Paris.

Feature 2

AHMEDABAD (IANS): All the state is a stage and all, well most, people in Gujarat turn dancers as Navratri begins on Thursday, heralding nine nights of music, colour and celebration in what is billed as the world's longest dance festival.

Navratri, literally translating to nine nights, is held during the first nine days of the Ashwin month of the Gujarati calendar.

The festival dedicated to goddess Durga combines the traditional with the modern in a seamless blend as the young and old gather to dance the 'garba' and the 'raas' to age-old songs and trendy chartbusters.

As bedtime gets extended to the early hours of the morning, dances are performed through the night at open grounds all over the state in grand evenings organised by local clubs or professional event managers.

In recent times, commercial organisers have stepped in to cash in on the popularity of the festival with garba programmes held at large arenas with hefty entry charges.

The commercial bashes started this year even before the beginning of Navratri, with two shows earlier this week, one each in Ahmedabad and Surat, by popular Mumbai-based singer Falguni Pathak.

Appearance matters, of course, and people make a beeline to shop for traditional costumes with elaborate embroidery and mirror work for women and the colourful 'kedia' costume for men.

Besides, crash courses in dancing are a hot favourite with youngsters who also make it to weight reduction clinics and beauty salons to look good during the nine days of partying.

The rampant commercialisation, with the increasing popularity of the festival, comes with its own share of problems.

Not everybody looks forward to Navratri revelries and citizens groups have opposed the high decibel song-and-dance routine that goes on all night.

Police in Ahmedabad have allowed garba programmes to go on till 1.30 a.m. after failed attempts last year to silence public address systems by midnight.

Authorities in Surat have enforced a deadline of midnight this year.

Police have made extra arrangements to avert any untoward incidents, particularly sexual harassment, during the festival.

Feature 3

RANCHI (IANS): For the last nine years, Ramashankar Prasad has never failed to perform an unusual ritual—keeping a pitcher filled with water on his chest for the nine days of the Navratri festival without letting a drop fall.

This time, Prasad has chosen the Lakshmi Narayan temple in Dhanbad district of Jharkhand as his venue to enact the act.

As hundreds flock to see his feat, this resident of Bihar's Arrah district lies still eating very little, happy simply to fulfil a promise made to the goddess.

He claims, "In 1996, Goddess Durga appeared to me and inspired me to observe this ritual for nine years. With her blessing, I have been able to keep up this tough practice."

For the nine days that he keeps the pitcher on his chest, Prasad survives on honey, basil leaves and a few drops of water from the Ganges river that Hindus consider holy.

This time, he will observe the ritual till October 22.

He has performed the prayer for eight years at different places in Bihar and Jharkhand. This is his ninth year.

"With the blessing of the goddess I have no problems in life. I have everything a person needs," Prasad said.

Asked if he would do it again next year, he said, "I am feeling relieved that I have kept up the ritual for nine years without a break and fulfilled my word.

I have not decided what to do next year. Everything will depend on the blessing of the goddess and my health condition."

Feature 4

CHENNAI (ENS): India is getting younger, what with roughly 55 per cent of its population estimated to be under 35 today. A preference for youthful things like fashionable clothes, speed machines and hi-tech gadgets is thus to be expected.

But, what could explain how something as formal as the office bag has also got younger, increasingly informal and colourful? According to industry sources, office luggage ac-counts for roughly 20 per cent of the Rs 500-crore luggage market in the country.

The metros and other big cities predictably account for the bulk of the market in value terms, largely on account of a higher level of consumerism and premium spend.

In comparison, Orissa is only a Rs 5-crore market for luggage, including unorganised sales. Yet, as a casual survey reveals, consumer preference in Bhubaneswar, a B class city, has also been getting younger in line with that elsewhere in the country.

For starters, the ubiquitous briefcase, once the only acceptable office luggage for men, is going out of circulation fast. According to industry sources, while briefcases accounted for almost 85 per cent of the market five years ago, today they have declined to 15 to 20 per cent, replaced by soft luggage that is both pleasing to the eyes and offer far greater flexibility and carrying comfort, thanks largely to the hands-free option they invariably offer.

As with all things, convenience has been a key driver for changes in the luggage space too, despite the fact that the category does not involve long pre-purchase considerations.

The manufacturers too seem to have realised the changing preference, though they haven't given up on briefcases yet. Leather bags are obviously hot, given the aesthetic possibilities and fashion appeal. Interestingly, however, it is nylon that's changing the face of the luggage industry with sales ranging from 300 to 1800 units. So much so that, while the premium end is still crowded with leather bags, there have been a number of nylon entries in the recent past.

Feature 5

THRISSUR (Kerala) (IANS): He is a vet, a dentist, a mahout and a sculptor all rolled into one — and Sankaranarayanan needs every one of those skills when he carves out tusks from softwood and fits them on elephants with nuts and bolts.

A mahout by profession, who has been working for the past 35 years with the famous Guruvayoor temple trust in southern India that owns 69 captive elephants, Sankaranarayanan started on this particular job only eight years ago.

"It was eight years ago when I first decided to experiment by making an artificial tusk for an elephant which had broken one of its tusks," the 63-year-old said.

It took long weeks and lots of work.

"I worked for close to three months with softwood and finally made a tusk. I fitted it with the help of nuts and bolts to the elephant's broken tusk," Sankaranarayanan told IANS.

Since then he has made artificial tusks for 10 elephants that he proudly says are better than the original.

While the natural tusk of an elephant weighs close to 50 kg, the artificial one weighs less than a kilo.

Explaining how he manages to fit the tusks, the mahout-dentist said: "I fix the tusk on to the broken piece of tusk or on the very small tusks of female elephants.

The skin is not pierced at all. It is a simple process of fitting it with bolts and nuts, much simpler than fixing an artificial tooth on human beings."

The most difficult task, he said, is not making the artificial tusk, which can take up to a month, but in finding the right kind of wood. Sankaranarayanan sources the precious wood from the forests of Trissur here.

But, yes, there is a rider. These tusks are essentially ornamental.

"I sell these tusks for just Rs.5,000 and they cannot be used for any sort of work. It can be used by the elephants when they join a temple festival. They add to the elephant's majestic looks," he said.

Magazine Headline Exercises

Exercise 1

Go through any two major news magazines available in your city. Compare the style adopted by them to write headlines.

Exercise 2

Write a headline for each of the following four articles using the following format:
Shoulder
Point Size: 12 caps
Number of letters: 16
Number of decks: 1

Main Headline
Point Size: 30 caps
Number of letters: 12
Number of decks:1

Strapline
Point Size: 14, upper-lower
Number of letters/decks: 60 letters spread across three decks

Report 1

NEW DELHI (IANS): Reader's Digest, among the world's most widely read magazines, has completed 50 years in India.

Loyal readers who have loved their monthly journey of laughter, drama, adventure and edification through the pages of this popular publication, can now look forward to the 50th anniversary issue featuring the best of Reader's Digest.

The collector's edition, set for December launch, will have a gold embossed hardbound jacket and is priced at Rs 49.50 for non-subscribers.

"It will have the choicest of everything that readers look forward to in the Digest — classic articles, word power, humour..." the publication's Manager said, adding that the content would be handpicked.

Some 250,000 copies of the collector's edition will be printed.

The world over, the magazine reaches almost 100 million people across 165 countries, and is read in 19 languages. The Digest has some 450,000 subscribers in India.

The magazine is relished for its simple style, with many true accounts running the gamut of human emotions and situations in life.

Report 2

NEW DELHI (PTI): The global bug has hit the Indian platter hard! *Dal-bhat* and *parathas* are fast doing a disappearing act with Thai and Chinese cuisine tantalising the taste buds of the average Indian. While for the connoisseurs, it is French all the way, Indian tastes are growing global and the trend is here to stay, predict the food gurus. No more are the Indians inclined to satiate their appetites with the traditional limited options and international cuisine has created a nichè in the desi palates, quite literally.

Led by the globetrotting genre, foodies here are not only more aware of the international food trends, but are also following the mantra of *dil maange more* sans any restrictions.

"International cuisine is fast becoming popular in India thanks to the jet-setting travellers. When they come back home they demand the same food that they had savoured elsewhere in the world", says Amit Choudhary, executive chef at a five-star hotel here.

The food preferences, however, vary and while an average Indian is going ga-ga over the Chinese and Thai cuisines, it is French or Italian for the more sophisticated palates. "Chinese were the first ones to make inroad into the burgeoning Indian food market but over the past decade Thai and Mexican cuisine has followed suit," says Rabindra Seth, noted travelogue and culinary writer.

Report 3

BANGALORE (ENS): Tom Cruise says in Top Gun: "I feel the need. The need for speed." Children too seem to feel the same way. Speed has become the key word upon which rests everything else.

Children these days seem to lack interest in most things and the few that grasp their attention get them hooked on to it for long.

Harry Potter, Pogo, Nickelodeon and Cartoon Network have become an integral part of every child's growing years. But these can be passed off as mild addictions when compared to the world of Nintendo and Play Stations that have created a larger-than-life image for this generation.

Games like Need For Speed and Road Rash have, to some extent, become a thing of the past. The craze for video games and collections have created quite a lot of hue and cry, especially among parents. They are the ones that end up ripping their pockets in an attempt to 'give their child everything' and in the process forget what is best for them.

"It is a common sight at home to see my children in front of the computer or the television. We always argue on the subject but nothing changes. It seems so hard to convince them to read a book or go out and play," says Mohan Prasad, a working professional. "Even when they talk among friends, it is only about how they out-score each other or find new techniques to beat their opponent in a video game", he adds.

Says Padma, "My 12-year-old son is quite addicted to video games and every month comes up with a new game to add to his collection. It's not easy to say no when they keep on persisting and at the end of it, you just want to get them off your back."

But is it worth it? Think about the extent to which your child can get affected when he is exposed to six-seven hours of Mortal Kombat, projecting a hero like Liu Kang or Johnny Cage, trying to win by endlessly kicking Raiden or Scorpion to death.

He develops a belief that being more violent makes him a winner and though virtual, it can leave quite an impression on your child's mind.

But this hasn't put an end to the production of such games. They have only increased in number and are available easily and quite abundantly in the market. It wasn't enough that games like Quake and Mortal Kombat have had a negative impact on children that we have new ones coming in every year.

Dragon Ball Z, Mortal Kombat Deception and Fire Fighters are just some of the names that children can expect this year.

Report 4

BANGALORE (ENS): It is widely believed that if a problem occurs, it is better to tackle it head on. The cast and crew of Dreamscope certainly seemed to take this approach when performing A R Gurney's Love Letters at Gallery Sumukha on October 28, for the drama started before the actual Drama.

A power cut moments before the action resulted in the actors improvising under candlelight to a reshuffled close-up audience in an unusual, intimate setting.

Challenging the background noise of a power generator without the aid of a microphone was no mean feat for the actors, so they should be commended for putting across the dialogue in a crystal clear fashion.

Love Letters surrounds two childhood friends, Andrew Makepeace Ladd III and Melissa Gardner, and their correspondence through their letters, as their lives take different courses over the span of 40 years. Of course, the couple fall in love and the tension between them through their written words is unbearable at times.

According to the author, Love Letters requires no actual stage, no rehearsal and no memorisation of lines from the actors. In many respects Gurney is spot on as the set is very minimal consisting of just a couple of tables and chairs and the actors simply read their 'letters' on stage.

However this doesn't mean that skilled acting is not required, as it must be very demanding for the two actors during the course of the performance, especially when they are the only actors involved and they don't interact with each other.

Brilliantly written, Gurney depicts the characters' personalities and feelings perfectly. But as important is what is not said in the letters, the feelings that aren't written but conveyed by the actors. It is the words between the lines that succors the development of the story and grips the audience.

Despite the technical difficulties, it was a pleasure to sit through the whole three hours of what must have been a very difficult performance for all involved.

7

DO'S AND DON'TS
THE 25 GOLDEN RULES

Headline writers need to look at their work as a craft that can only be learnt the hard way. Fortunately, over the decades desk veterans have come up with several do's and don'ts that have now become the unwritten rules of headline writing. The following are a set of 25 golden rules of headline writing that has been arrived at, modified and passed on by one generation of headline writers to another:

RULE 1: SIMPLE AND SHORT WORDS

The first pre-requisite of any good headline is the use of simple words, words that are easily understood by the common reader. There was all round shock and horror when the news broke that over 50 school children had been burnt alive in a fire in a Kumbakonam school. The headline writer of a Tamil Nadu newspaper used the word 'conflagration' to show the magnitude of the fire and the havoc it caused. But 'conflagration' is not a commonly used word. A simpler and a more powerful word was 'fire'. Also, the verb 'perish' could have been substituted with the shorter word 'die'.

Original
50 children perish in Kumbakonam conflagration
Revised
50 children die in Kumbakonam school fire

The headline writer could also have used action verbs *burnt alive* instead of neutral verb *die* to underscore the horror.

50 children burnt alive in Kumbakonam school fire

RULE 2: CONCRETE WORDS

The headline writer must avoid generalizations and select words that are specific and concrete. A headline where specific words made a world of difference was about the tragic death of four Bangalore engineers who drowned in a lake. The headline writer glossed over the identity of the engineers while writing the headline.

Original
Four professionals drown in lake
Revised
4 Bangalore engineers drown in lake

Similarly, there was shock and outrage in 2004 when a Mumbai actress who was working in a Maithili language film in Bihar complained that the film's director and actors had sexually assaulted her. The news agency, which moved the story, gave the following headline:

Actress cries sexual harassment

The headline summarized the main point of the story but it left the reader wondering where the incident had occurred. The headline was modified by the Newindpress.com desk which added the name of the state where the incident had occurred and also gave an identity to the actress without naming her.

Mumbai actress sexually assaulted in Bihar

There is little doubt that concrete words give strength to a headline. Examinations generate scores of stories about the ingenuity of students in cheating. Some students write answers on strips of paper and then hide them among their clothes, some seek the help of invigilators to answer papers, some smuggle answer sheets outside the examination hall and some intimidate teachers and merrily cheat. There have been instances of brothers or sisters answering the examination for their less endowed kin with or without the help of school authorities.

These reports get pushed to inside pages of newspapers once the annual 'exam fever' subsides. But one report that came from Jammu was a stunner. It spoke of a father who paid Rs 1 lakh to a Bihari girl to appear for the medical entrance test in place of his daughter. Unfortunately, the headline did not mention the amount paid to the girl for her services. Nor did it mention the name of the exam. As a result, the headline failed to grab attention.

Original
Father arranges test by proxy for daughter
Revised
Father pays Rs 1 lakh to girl to write medical entrance test for daughter

RULE 3: AVOID MODIFIERS

A common misconception is that adjectives and adverbs add colour to a headline. They do not. Instead they eat up valuable headline space.

B K Chaturvedi takes over as *new* cabinet secretary

The adjective 'new' could easily have been avoided. It does not add anything new to the headline.

But a headline that suffered on account of an adjective was the one that was related to India-Pakistan talks (Fig. 7.1). Every Indian knows that talks between India and Pakistan are a round-the-year phenomenon. Sometimes they break down, sometimes they pick up speed. But one thing is for certain. There is no flippancy about the efforts that are made by both sides to have the talks going. It was therefore amusing to read a headline that said:

India, Pak to continue serious talks

Surely, the talks could not have been for fun.

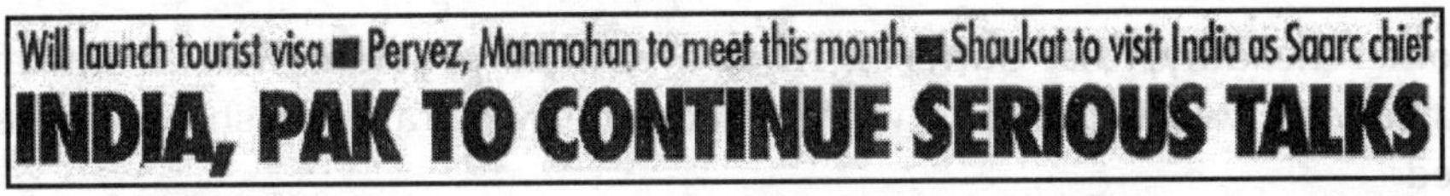

Will launch tourist visa ■ Pervez, Manmohan to meet this month ■ Shaukat to visit India as Saarc chief

INDIA, PAK TO CONTINUE SERIOUS TALKS

Fig. 7.1: *An unnecessary adjective – serious – used in an* Asian Age *headline on India-Pakistan talks.*

RULE 4: SELECT WORDS CAREFULLY

The strength of a headline depends on the words chosen by the headline writer. A good headline may be ruined if a wrong or inappropriate word has been used. All headline writers need to guard against the following four errors.

Inappropriate Words

The worst headlines are those where wrong words are used. A headline writer in Lucknow chose the word 'mania' to describe the state of mind of bureaucrats when the Mayawati government came to power in the state. Mania refers to obsession, desire, craze, a fad or passion. Surely, none of these words reflect the feeling of insecurity that overtakes bureaucrats when a new government assumes office. A more appropriate word would have been 'fear'.

Inappropriate: **Transfer** mania **haunts UP officials**
Appropriate: **Transfer** fear **haunts UP officials**

There was reason to rejoice when Zodiac Clothing Company of Mumbai acquired a Dubai-based shirt firm. However, the *Economic Times* headline writer took part of the punch away by choosing the wrong verb (Fig. 7.2).

Zodiac seizes **Dubai**
shirt firm for Rs 25 cr

Zodiac seizes Dubai shirt firm for Rs 25 cr

Textile Cos Scramble To Go Global Ahead Of Quota Expiry

Fig. 7.2: *An* Economic Times *headline where the wrong verb 'seizes' was used. The correct verb would have been 'acquires' or 'buys'. Also, the headline suffers from a bad break. The first deck gives the impression that Zodiac has seized Dubai.*

Another headline that suffered from a similar problem was about an accident involving two trains. The writer made the two trains crash when they had collided.

275 killed as trains crash **near Saharanpur**

Another headline where the writer went overboard was the one related to a story where a Welshman put his wife's brain on sale on the auction site ebay. The story lead was straight and to the point. It read:

LONDON: Believe it or not! A Welsh surveyor placed an ad on auction website eBay, putting his very much alive wife's brain on sale.

The reporter wanted to stress on the fact that the woman was not dead by using the phrase 'very much alive'. There was nothing wrong in the usage. In fact, it made the lead vibrant. However, the effect was not the same when the headline writer wrote:

Man puts alive wife's brain on sale

It was a wrong word to use and it undid the reporter's good work. The adjective that should have been used was 'living'.

Man puts living wife's brain on sale

Or better still, the headline writer should have stuck to the simple noun and verb in writing the headline. The story needed no embellishments. It was so bizarre that it brought a smile without any modifiers.

Straight headline: *Welshman puts wife's brain on sale*

Malapropisms

Sometimes, under pressure, headline writers choose wrong words because they sound alike. These confusing words cause much embarrassment, sometimes even hilarity, on news desks. A headline that caused much merriment related to the Staines murder case.

A day before an Orissa court was to announce its sentence to those who were convicted in the Staines murder case the state police, fearing tension, stepped up security around churches. The headline writer wrote:

Security heightened **for Orissa churches**

The verb that should have been used was 'tightened' instead of 'heightened'.

Typos

The word may be right, but the meaning may be distorted because of an unexpected typing error, commonly referred to as typo. There were several red faces in a Lucknow newspaper when the headline for the traditional meeting between the Governor and the city's editors went thus:

Governor provides *erotic* food to city editors

The food was 'exotic', not 'erotic'.

Confusing Constructions

Sometimes headline constructions convey a wrong meaning. One headline that needed to be rewritten was for the storming of a Russian school (Fig. 7.3). The headline used in the Chennai edition of the *New Indian Express* read:

Rebels storm school,
take over 400 hostage

The headline was not wrong, but it needed careful reading to understand what the headline writer wanted to convey. The first reaction on reading the headline was one of confusion because the verb 'take' was used next to the adjective 'over'. They were read as one word 'takeover', which has a completely different meaning.

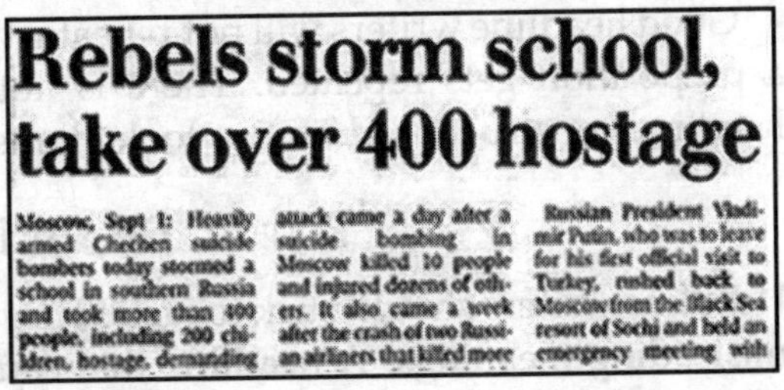

Rebels storm school, take over 400 hostage

Moscow, Sept 1: Heavily armed Chechen suicide bombers today stormed a school in southern Russia and took more than 400 people, including 200 children, hostage, demanding attack came a day after a suicide bombing in Moscow killed 10 people and injured dozens of others. It also came a week after the crash of two Russian airliners that killed more

Russian President Vladimir Putin, who was to leave for his first official visit to Turkey, rushed back to Moscow from the Black Sea resort of Sochi and held an emergency meeting with

Fig. 7.3: *A headline run in the* New Indian Express *where the meaning got clouded.*

Rule 5: Avoid Repetition of Words

A question that is often asked is: should words be repeated in a headline? The answer is no. The 2004 India-Pakistan cricket series was hailed as historic because it was held after a period of 15 years. The fact that India won the series 2-1 made it even more historic because it was the first time that India beat Pakistan, in Pakistan. Further, the fact that India had won a test series abroad after a gap of 11 years made it even sweeter.

All these firsts must have put great pressure on the headline writer who chose to stress the historic part by using the word twice in the headline.

Historic win by Team India in historic series

But was it necessary to use the word 'historic' twice? Would it not have been enough to use the word once?

Team India wins historic series

Another headline featuring the Indian cricket team also had a repetition of a word (Fig. 7.4). The headline was written for the news report stating that the Indian team—popularly known as Men in Blue on account of their blue uniform for one-day internationals—had been knocked out of the ICC Champions Trophy.

Knock-out blues for the Men in Blue

Fig. 7.4: *A headline run in the* Hindustan Times *where a word was repeated without adding value to it.*

Good headline writers will not repeat words. However, there may be times when a preposition gets repeated. There is nothing wrong in it as long as the basic headline construction does not look clumsy.

Rule 6: Do not Imply Meanings

Headline writers should stick to facts. They should not draw conclusions or convey misleading meanings. A headline that caused much unpleasantness was the one written about a passenger dying in an airplane. The aircraft was removed to the parking bay in Mumbai after the passengers disembarked. However, the cabin crew failed to notice a man who had died. This was surely an example of negligence on the part of airlines staff, but the headline writer stretched the meaning:

Body left to stink in aircraft

The headline implied that the body had been left behind on purpose. It was sensational; but was it factual? No. Headlines like this give a newspaper a bad name; often they land newspapers in legal trouble.

Even worse is to mislead the readers. An indefensible headline was the one written on US President George Bush's reaction to the film titled *Osama*. The headline implied that Bush was praising Osama bin Laden, America's most wanted man after the 9/11 terror attack, though Bush had praised the film by that name.

The headline writer placed the name Osama in single quotes to indicate that this Osama was different from the terrorist Osama. But this at best can be described as a fig leaf to cover a serious ethical crime. Not even the exclamation mark could save the headline from being called a rank bad headline.

Bush showers praise on 'Osama'!

Washington (ANI): Think US President George W Bush could ever shower praises on his number one enemy—Osama bin Laden?

Yes, and it happened on Monday, when he called upon the governors of different states to watch the film 'Osama'. According to a report in The Daily Times, the President told the nation's governors: 'You ought to see the movie Osama. It's an interesting movie. It talks about what it was like to be a woman in Afghanistan during the Taliban era.'

Another indefensible headline was the one that stated:

Salman and Aishwarya have a date

The headline conveyed the impression that the Hindi film industry's leading stars were all set for a reconciliation date—after their great spat that had the industry in turmoil for quite some time. But this was not the case. The date was not a rapprochement appointment set up by the two stars. Instead, the term 'date' referred to the release date of their films *Kyon, Ho Gaya Na* starring Aishwarya Rai and *Phir Milenge* starring Salman Khan. By sheer coincidence the two films were being released on the same date. A more appropriate headline would have been:

Salman, Aishwarya starrers being released on the same date

Rule 7: Use Verbs

In newspaper jargon a headline without verbs is referred to as a label head, and not wrongly. Such headlines convey no meaning. Look at the following two headlines, one with a verb and the other without one.

IA fares
IA hikes fares

The first headline is incomplete. It does not inform the reader about the action taken by Indian Airlines regarding fares. The reader needs to go through the story to learn that Indian Airlines has announced an increase in fares. In contrast, the second headline is complete because the verb 'hikes' tells the reader what has happened to the fares.

Another headline that went flat on account of a missing verb was the one related to the upgradation of facilities in government hospitals' anaesthesia departments in Tamil Nadu. The headline writer wrote:

Anaesthesia upgrade at govt hospitals

In contrast, the headline acquired a clear and sharp meaning when the word upgrade was used as a verb.

Anaesthesia departments being upgraded in govt hospitals

RULE 8: USE VERBS CORRECTLY

Headlines lose rhythm when the verbs are used in an inappropriate manner. A classic example is the use of the word 'raid'. It is used both as a noun and as a verb. Both forms are popular with headline writers. But sometimes the writers trip as happened with this headline that was run in the Chennai edition of the *New Indian Express*:

CBI raids on Maya's houses

The headline was built on a preposition. This was not a good option. It weakened the headline immediately. The headline would have become stronger if the word 'raids' had been used as a verb.

Corrected headline: **CBI raids Maya's houses**

The same day, the *Hindu* used the word 'raids' as a noun. However, its headline conveyed more meaning because it used the verb 'conducts' to indicate what had happened.

The *Hindu* headline: ***CBI conducts raids on Mayawati's residences***

RULE 9: PLACE VERBS AHEAD OF NOUNS

It is not enough to use a verb in a headline, it is also important to ensure that it follows a noun. The headlines where the verb follows the noun are less abrupt as is evident from the following examples.

Original
Showcasing India's achievements
Revised
India showcases its achievements

Original
Axing of Agarkar was avoidable: ex-players
Revised
Agarkar's axing was avoidable: ex-players

RULE 10: AVOID USE OF AUXILIARY VERBS

The use of auxiliary verbs 'is/are' and their past tense forms should be avoided. This is because the space saved by dropping the verbs 'is/are' — whose use is implied — can be used to add a more relevant word.

During the 2004 Lok Sabha election campaign, much heat was generated over a sari distribution function that led to the death of several women in a stampede in Lucknow. The opposition wanted the Election Commission to probe the tragedy. Since Lucknow happened to be the constituency of the then Prime Minister, Mr Atal Behari Vajpayee, the BJP President summoned a press conference to deflect the opposition charges.

His statement that the opposition was politicizing the stampede went as the headline in several newspapers. However, the auxiliary verb 'is' was not used as it was not required.

Auxiliary verb (is) is implied: **Opposition politicising stampede, says Venkaiah**

However, there are two exceptions to this rule. One, an auxiliary verb should be used if it helps in balancing the different decks of a headline.

First deck is shorter
**Opposition politicising
stampede, says Venkaiah**

Both decks are equal
**Opposition *is* politicising
stampede, says Venkaiah**

Two, auxiliary verbs should not be dropped if the headline becomes incomplete without them. A good example of this is a quote that was run as a headline.

'All they talk about is Sonia, caste, cows'

Here the use of the auxiliary verb 'is' is a must.

Rule 11: Do not Use Articles

Like the auxiliary verbs, the use of articles—a, an and the—is also implied in a headline. The articles should be used only in those rare cases where the headline would look awkward without them, as for instance in this headline:

Now, Atal calls Modi issue a thing of past

The statement was made by former Prime Minister, Mr Atal Behari Vajpayee, on the eve of a crucial BJP Parliamentary Board meeting in 2004 to discuss the fate of the then Gujarat Chief Minister, Mr Narendra Modi. Mr Vajpayee in his comments said that the issue of Modi's removal was 'a thing of the past.'

However, the headline writer removed the article 'a' from the phrase making the headline look awkward.

Now, Atal calls Modi issue thing of past

Headline writers should not drop those articles from phrases that may lead to an unintended change in meaning. A headline where the entire meaning changed was the one related to Indian cricket captain Sourav Ganguly's comments on India's celebrated fast bowler Srinath after the latter had retired. The headline was based on a comment that appeared in the last paragraph of a PTI story that was moved during the historic India-Pakistan series.

NEW DELHI (PTI) : Indian cricket captain Sourav Ganguly has conceded that the declaration in the Multan Test against Pakistan with Sachin Tendulkar on 194 was a 'mistake'.

Asked what he felt made the present team different from the past sides, he said, "We have some exceptionally talented players and we have managed to groom them. The commitment level is high and work ethics are there for you to see… The support group has played its role in the improvement and I must say the role played by (coach) John Wright has been outstanding."

Ganguly also said that seniors in the team had made his job easy although he did have some problems with now retired medium pacer Javagal Srinath.

"The seniors have made my job easy. I had a few problems with Srinath. He had his own views on certain aspects of our approach but then his intentions were always to serve the team better. Believe me, the seniors in the team have been my strength."

The headline writer picked up this sensational point and wrote:

I had few problems with Srinath: Ganguly

The headline implied that Ganguly had hardly any problems with Srinath. On the contrary, what the Indian captain said was that he had some problems as becomes clear from the revised headline that carries the article 'a'.

I had a few problems with Srinath: Ganguly

Do's and Don'ts

Rule 12: Use Abbreviations Carefully

When it comes to writing headlines, abbreviations are both a boon and a bane. On the one hand, they make it possible to provide more information in a headline but on the other they obscure meaning especially when they are not well known. There are four points that need to be kept in mind when using abbreviations in headlines.

Abbreviating Words

There are several words whose abbreviated forms have been accepted as headlinese. Thus, administration has become 'admn', government has been shortened to 'govt' and secretary has been reduced to 'secy'. These words were abbreviated because they were used frequently in headlines and occupied considerable space. Today, they are well accepted as headlinese.

A latest entry to the ranks of headlinese is 'Finmin'. The business papers have always struggled to put Finance Ministry in the headline despite most stories requiring its use. They have therefore coined their own word—a word that is becoming more popular than the original.

However, the same cannot be said of 'mkt', which newspapers have now started using as the abbreviated form of market, or 'distt' as the abbreviated form of district. Unfortunately, Indian headline writers are revelling in this trend because they find it a convenient way of getting around headline blues.

A popular usage these days is of the American slang 'Prez' for President. Most Indian newspapers find this a convenient way of referring to President in headlines. It may even become headlinese after continued use; but today it surely looks like an eyesore. Another eyesore is the shortening of the word through to 'thru' (Fig. 7.5).

Chennai airport development thru jt venture route planned

Fig. 7.5: *The word through has been truncated to 'thru' in this* Business Line *headline.*

Another unfortunate development in Indian newspapers is the abbreviation of the names of cities and states to meet headline requirements. Thus, Maharashtra has become 'M'rashtra' and 'Hyderabad' has become 'H'bad'. A good headline writer must avoid short cuts in writing headlines.

Interchangeable Abbreviations

Another difficulty arises when abbreviations are interchangeable. Thus, EC stands for Election Commission as also European Community, and WB refers to both West Bengal and World Bank. Such abbreviations should either be avoided or written in a context where their meaning becomes clear.

Excessive Use of Abbreviations

A headline suffers if the editor uses too many abbreviations to convey meaning.

SC issues notice to IOA, WFI

Abbreviating Names

The editors should also be careful about names. It is important that only those names are used in the abbreviated form that are popularly accepted and well known. Good examples are MGR, NTR, Big B and Ash.

Some names become popular because of their frequent use in the media. When R. Venkataraman became the President, headline writers came up with the abbreviation RV. The same thing happened with P.V.Narasimha Rao; he was referred to as PVN when he was the Prime Minister. However, once these two distinguished leaders demitted office, news reports about them dwindled in number and frequency. The recall value of RV and PVN went down. It therefore became necessary to refer to them by their full names than by their abbreviated names.

RULE 13: BE CAREFUL WHILE COINING SOBRIQUETS

The media should be careful in baptizing public figures. When the celebrated economist Dr Manmohan Singh became the Prime Minister, the headline writers chose to use the address 'Doctor'. This was in recognition of the fact that Dr Manmohan Singh had a doctorate in Economics and was very different from the run of the mill politicians.

The same happened to India's cricket captain Sourav Ganguly. The media latched on to the term *dada* that was being used by Ganguly's younger teammates as an affectionate form of address. (Incidentally, the term *dada* is used to address elders in Ganguly's home state West Bengal.)

Another Indian cricketer who is well known by his sobriquet is Rahul Dravid. The sobriquet — The Wall — was used as a recognition of Rahul Dravid's immaculate defence technique. It has now become a part of headlinese.

'*Behenji*' is another sobriquet that the media now uses for the Bahujan Samaj Party leader, Ms Mayawati. Like *Dada*, *Behenji* too is a respectful form of address used to refer to elder sisters in several north Indian states.

Rule 14: How to Use Attribution

One of the primary tenets of good journalism is to source reports to individuals and organizations. This gives the news reports an identifiable face, and lends credence to the comments and statements made in the report. The same principle applies to headlines. All headlines that are sourced to individuals or organizations enjoy greater acceptability as compared to those that are used without attribution.

However, it is not possible to use attribution in all headlines. Also, for attribution to be meaningful it is essential that the individual, functionary or organization making the statement should be well known (see also Chapter 4). The following rules explain the points that need to be kept in mind when using attribution.

When the Individual is Well Known

Celebrities like film stars, sportsmen, politicians etc., need no second introduction. Their statements can be directly attributed to them. For instance, when the BJP-led NDA threatened to boycott the Budget session of Parliament in 2004 over the sacking of four Governors and the presence of 'tainted' ministers, Prime Minister Manmohan Singh offered to discuss and resolve all issues peacefully. The *Hindu* headlined the story as:

All issues can be discussed: Manmohan

The attribution could also have been Prime Minister or PM or Doctor. However, it could not have been Singh, because Singh is a common surname. In Dr Manmohan Singh's cabinet itself there are several Singhs, the most notable being Mr Arjun Singh. The reader would therefore have ended up getting confused if the surname Singh was used.

In some cases an individual may be well known both by his first name and surname. Good examples are Atal Behari Vajpayee, George Fernandes, Uma Bharati. In such cases, editors need to step in and decide which part of the individual's name will be used as attribution in the headline to ensure consistency in usage.

When the Individual is Better Known by Designation

Several news reports are sourced to officials who make a statement in the course of their duty. For instance, when the Central Bureau of Investigation official heading the stamp paper scam held a press conference to state that several important people were involved in the scam, the headline writer correctly attributed the statement to CBI instead of the official's name, since few people would have known the CBI official by name.

Several VIPs involved in stamp paper scam: CBI official

When a Statement is Made on Behalf of Political Parties or Government Departments

All major parties use articulate leaders to brief the press on the stands taken by their respective organizations. Similarly, a senior official in the Ministry of External Affairs briefs the press on the positions adopted by the Government of India on different issues. The statements made by these individuals are attributed to the organizations they represent.

BJP accuses UPA of confrontation
India not to seek Israeli arms

In the first headline, the party name BJP is used instead of the spokesperson's name; similarly, in the second headline the statement is referred to India and not to the spokesperson who spoke on behalf of the Government of India.

When a Functionary Makes a Statement of Fact

Attribution is not needed when a statement of fact is made, be it related to the action of police or to a public event. It is therefore not necessary to indicate the government agency that increased the petrol price by one rupee or fixed the dates of university examinations. The same holds true of a statement made by the government.

Madras University exams from Dec 1
Petrol prices go up by 1 rupee
Talks with Pak successful

RULE 15: ENSURE THAT HEADLINES ARE VISUALLY PLEASING

The first attribute of a good headline is to communicate; the second is to make the page look visually pleasing. A headline writer must ensure that all decks in a headline are equal; if that is difficult to achieve then the first deck must be the longest (see Chapter 1). Any multideck headline looks like an eyesore where the second or third deck is longer than the first deck.

Two visually pleasing headlines are:

TN CM seeks PM's help
to resolve water crisis

10 killed as
Naxals raze
police posts

The following headlines need to be rewritten:

**No hike in
passenger fares**

**Vajpayee
to meet Musharraf
in US**

Another principle that flows from this rule is that headlines must run across their full width. White holes on either side of the headlines do not reflect well on news desks (Fig. 7.6).

A touching gesture by Kalam

Fig. 7.6: *A headline that was centred in the* Hindu *and which left a lot of white space on both the sides.*

RULE 16: ENSURE THAT EACH DECK WORKS AS A UNIT

This is one rule that is rarely followed in Indian newspapers. It is common to come across headlines where the designation is run across two lines or a prepositional phrase is run across two decks. A few language newspapers even break names. This is in sharp contrast to the American and British newspapers where each deck in a headline is treated as one complete unit.

Headline writers may argue that they are under great pressure and that trying to write each line as a complete unit is a slow and tortuous process. But a good newspaper is one that pays attention to such minor details. It would not have allowed the name Karan Singh (Fig. 7.7) to be broken or the award name

Akan D Emil Award (Fig. 7.8) run in two lines as happened in the Bangalore edition of the *Asian Age*. The headline was not wrong, but perfection was missing. A little effort could have given the headline more grace.

Karan Singh new Auroville chairman

By Our Correspondent

New Delhi, Sept. 21: As part of the ongoing "detoxification" campaign started by Union human resources development minister Arjun Singh, Congress leader and Rajya Sabha MP Karan Singh

Fig. 7.7: *The name Karan Singh was run across two decks in the* Asian Age.

Ex-Isro chief gets Alan D Emil Award

Bangalore: Former Isro chairman K. Kasturirangan has been conferred the prestigious Alan D Emil memorial award for international cooperation by the Paris-based International Astronautical Federation.

Fig. 7.8: *The award name* Alan D Emil Award *was broken in the* Asian Age *headline.*

To ensure that the line and thought break together the headline writer needs to watch for three things.

Verb Phrase

All efforts must be made to run the verb phrase in the same deck.

Original
Drying of lake drives away birds

Revised
Birds keep away from dry lake

Adjectival/Adverbial Phrases

Modifiers that are part of an adjectival or adverbial phrase must be run in the same deck. They should not be delinked from the words they seek to modify. Sometimes, this also helps in removing ambiguity that a bad break may introduce.

Protests over petrol price hike continue

The first line indicates that the protests were over petrol though in reality they were over the increase in the price of petrol. The headline should have been modified as:

No let up in protests over petrol price hike

Such breaks look particularly ugly when they break words that are read as one on account of usage even though they may be two words. When Bangalore City Corporation resolved to build seven overbridges, the *Asian Age* ran the following headline (Fig. 7.9):

**7 foot over
bridges to
combat
city traffic**

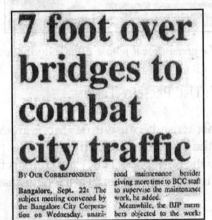

**7 foot over
bridges to
combat
city traffic**

BY OUR CORRESPONDENT

Bangalore, Sept. 22: The subject meeting convened by the Bangalore City Corporation on Wednesday, unani-

road maintenance beside giving more time to BCC staff to supervise the maintenance work, he added.

Meanwhile, the BJP members objected to the work.

Fig. 7.9: *An awkward headline run by the* Asian Age *on the building of seven overbridges in Bangalore.*

Prepositional phrases

These are the most difficult to handle, and invariably cause the maximum problems. Extra care therefore needs to be taken when writing a headline that has a prepositional phrase.

**ICICI mops
up Rs 400 cr**

Instead of using a prepositional phrase in two lines this headline could have been corrected using a verb.

**ICICI raises
Rs 400 crore**

Sometimes the break in prepositional phrase is so abrupt that it makes the entire headline look awkward. This is what happened to a headline that was run in the *Hindustan Times* following a flood alert on the banks of Sutlej river (Fig. 7.10):

**High alert, evacuation
on along Sutlej banks**

High alert, evacuation on along Sutlej banks

Rajnish Sharma
New Delhi, August 10

THE CENTRE asked the Himachal Pradesh government on Tuesday to evacuate all villages close to the banks of the Sutlej after China said it could not drain water from the rising which has a checkpost on the Sino-Indian border from where the lake can be seen.

Satellite images given to the Disaster Management Cell by the National Remote Sensing Agency show the lake has grown from about 1.9 km in length to 4.7 km. Its width is the same as earlier.

Flood threat

Fig. 7.10: *A headline with a bad break of a prepositional phrase in the* Hindustan Times.

RULE 17: USE PRESENT TENSE

A news report is written in the past tense because it describes an event that has already occurred. Headlines, on the contrary, are written in the present tense because they provide immediacy to the newspaper. They also impart freshness and help save space because most past tense forms of verbs are longer than the present tense forms.

Present tense
Home Minister defends US offer
Past tense
Home Minister defended US offer

Present tense
Manmohan heaps scorn on Opposition
Past tense
Manmohan heaped scorn on Opposition

Quite clearly, the past tense forms make headlines stale and convey a feeling that the news report is talking about an event that occurred long ago.

Even more serious is the use of two different forms of tense in a headline. This mistake was made in the story on Dhananjoy Chatterjee, a convict who had filed a mercy petition before the President of India and had also simultaneously appealed to the Supreme Court. However, the Supreme Court declined to entertain the petition of Chatterjee—facing execution for the rape and murder of a 14-year-old girl—stating that the President was already examining the subject. The headline became indefensible because the writer used both the present and past tense forms of verbs.

Original

Dhananjoy's fate hangs **as SC** declined **to entertain mercy petition**

Revised

Dhananjoy's fate hangs **as SC** declines **to entertain mercy petition**

For events that are to take place in the future the infinitive form of the verb should be used.

Bill on AIDS to be tabled next week

Govt. will hike petrol prices soon

RULE 18: USE OF PUNCTUATION MARKS

Punctuation marks should be used sparingly in a headline because a headline, by its very definition, is a skeletonized sentence. Too many punctuation marks blur meaning as happened with this anchor headline used by *The Indian Express* (Fig. 7. 11).

World baby boom now regional, read: India, Pak

Fig. 7.11: *Two commas and one colon in the space of three words cloud meaning in a headline used in the* Indian Express.

However, different newspapers follow different style rules regarding punctuation marks. The following are some broad do's and don'ts regarding punctuation marks.

Full Stop

The full stop must be avoided as far as possible and definitely should not be used at the end of the headline. This is because full stops block headline space equivalent to a letter. Also, too many full stops reduce the page's visual appeal.

Full stops should, however, be used in very special cases. One, when a headline is made of two full sentences, as in a quotation. Then the first sentence can end with a full stop. Two, when a newspaper style requires full stops to be used with acronyms (Fig. 7.12).

A brilliant example of the use of full stop was in a headline written by the *Indian Express* when the first bus rolled on the Srinagar-Muzzaffarabad route after half a

Religious freedom in India has improved: U.S. report

By Sridhar Krishnaswami   more inclusive rhetoric regard-   dia) has already taken some   cials have also urged that the

Fig. 7.12: *The full stop used with the abbreviation U.S. in the* Hindu.

century. It was a historic occasion, and the newspaper broke new ground in headline writing (Fig. 7.13).

Fig. 7.13: *A brilliant headline written on the historic start of the bus service from Srinagar to Muzzaffarabad. The headline broke tradition by using full stops.*

Comma

Comma plays a special role in headlines. It is often used in place of *and* as it saves space.

Mulayam and Advani to visit UP

To make the headline fit in the available space, the headline writer substituted the conjunction *and* with a comma, and saved space equivalent to two letters.

Mulayam, Advani to visit UP

However, care must be exercised in using commas. Misplaced commas can play havoc with the meaning of the headline, as do missing commas.

Gowda favours BJP	Gowda favours BJP,	Gowda favours, BJP
flays CPM call	flays CPM call	flays CPM call

The first headline that carries no commas is grammatically incorrect; the second headline gives the impression that Gowda favours the opposition Bharatiya Janata Party and not his alliance partner CPM which is factually incorrect; the third headline is the correct one, where the comma clears the confusion. Gowda is clearly favouring the CPM call while the BJP is attacking it.

Colon

A colon is often used in place of the attributive verb as it saves space.

Original headline
Centre eager to hold polls in October, asserts Jaitley
Revised headline
Centre eager to hold polls in October: Jaitley

However, colons should not be used to introduce a subject. They make headlines look awkward and clumsy. As far as possible, a headline should be built around a single thought that is complete in itself. The headline about the Tamil Nadu government planning fresh operations against Veerappan lost its meaning when the headline writer used the colon to anchor the headline. The same happened to the headline on the protest motion moved by the Opposition on the subject of tainted ministers.

Veerappan: TN to launch new operations
Tainted ministers: Opposition moves protest motion

Also, a colon should not be used to connect two separate clauses. Arjun Singh, when he became the Human Resources Minister in the Congress-led UPA government, reversed several decisions that had been taken by his immediate predecessor Murli Manohar Joshi. However, one decision that Arjun Singh decided to uphold was the hiring of Urdu teachers. This incidentally was a promise that the previous Prime Minister Atal Behari Vajpayee had made. The headline writer needed to bring out this interesting aspect. Unfortunately, the headline writer chose to use two clauses with a colon providing the connection. The headline would have looked much better if a comma with an appropriate verb had been used.

Original
Arjun to fulfil Vajpayee promise: 1.20 lakh Urdu teachers
Revised
Arjun to fulfil Vajpayee promise, hire 1.20 lakh Urdu teachers

Semi-colon

Semi-colons are frequently used in headlines. They are more useful than colons when separating two related points. A good example of the use of semi-colon is the headline written on the induction of Maqbool Dar in the Union cabinet and the elevation of Beni Prasad as a cabinet minister.

Dar inducted as home minister;
Beni Prasad gets cabinet rank

Long Dash/Hyphen

The long dash is generally avoided in most newspapers, as it does not look visually pleasing (Fig. 7.14).

Fig. 7.14: *The long dash used in a headline in the* Indian Express.

Hyphens must be used with adjectival phrases.

5-year-old boy falls in well

Hyphens should not be dropped in words where hyphenation gives a new meaning to a word. The story about a man-eater turned hilarious when the headline writer inadvertently dropped the hyphen.

Man eater roams Kheri forests

Exclamation Mark

Exclamation marks should be used sparingly in headlines. They should be used only when there is strong irony in a story or an unexpected twist. For instance, few readers would expect the actor who plays the role of Spiderman in the film of that name to be scared of heights. The very nature of the role requires the actor to be ready to jump from heights—of course, in a way that it does not endanger his life. The use of the exclamation mark in the following Spiderman story was therefore appropriate.

Spiderman is scared of heights!

WASHINGTON (ANI): 'Spiderman' actor Tobey Maguire has revealed that he suffers from acrophobia, that is, he is scared of heights. According to Star magazine, Tobey has admitted that he is extremely scared of standing on the ledge of a building and looking down, but does not mind swinging from ropes.

Exclamation marks can also be used for headlining humorous stories. The headline writer scored a perfect ten with this headline about two calves who were married in an Orissa village.

Moo! Bovine couple tie nuptial knot in style

Quotation Marks

Single quote marks should be used for both partial and full quotes. Once again, the reasoning is the saving of space and visual appeal. However, one newspaper that used both single and double quote marks in headlines before it went in for a redesign was the *Hindu* (Figs 7.15 and 7.16). Most other newspapers prefer to use single quote marks only.

'U.S. raised Gujarat riots with BJP-led Government'

By Sridhar Krishnaswami

WASHINGTON, SEPT. 15. The United States had raised the issue tians or others. There's certainly a rise in cases of attacks on Hindus and other minority reli- "... the pogroms in Gujarat, for example, were not carried out by the Central Govern-

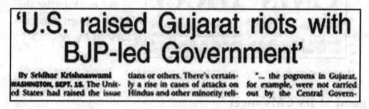

Fig. 7.15: *A headline from the* Hindu *using a single quote.*

"NSSP: U.S., India interests in action"

By Matthew S. Borman

In the article entitled, "India, U.S. & Trade in Technology" * Removing the Indian Space Research Organisation (ISRO) headquarters from the Department of Commerce's Entity List ing the time and uncertainty of such requirements. The current high volume of such license applications (about 250 in fiscal the September 22 Federal Register notice. A second Federal Register notice was published on Wednesday, September 29.

Fig. 7.16: *Another headline from the* Hindu *where a double quote mark has been used. Clearly, double quote marks take more space and look less appealing.*

Care should, however, be taken not to use too many quote marks in a headline. They cause confusion.

Rule 19: Use of Apostrophes

Wrong usage of an apostrophe can introduce unnecessary errors in a headline. The most common mistake happens with the singular and plural forms of nouns.

An apostrophe need not be used with plural nouns when they are used in the abbreviated form, unless the writer wants to turn the word into a possessive case. An example of this error occurred in the headline that was written for the appeal made by the Indian President, Mr Abdul Kalam, to members of Parliament during the second half of 2003. The headline writer placed the apostrophe before the letter 's' in the abbreviation MPs. The headline, as a result, conveyed the impression that the appeal was addressed to a single MP.

Headline used: **Get real, Kalam's second message to MP's**
Revised: **Get real, Kalam's second message to MPs**

When a word or an acronym used in the possessive case ends in the letter 's', there is no need to use an apostrophe after 's' (Fig. 7.17). The stress is understood, and the headline writer saves space.

Fig. 7.17: *Apostrophe is not needed after the letter* **s** *when a word is used in the possessive case.*

Preferable
BJP feels good at its CMs meet
Avoid
BJP feels good at its CMs' meet

RULE 20: AVOID OVERLOADING

Headlines that seek to highlight more than one point should be avoided. They leave the reader confused because the headline writer uses abbreviations and takes liberties with grammar to squeeze more information.

When militancy was at its height in Kashmir, news reports filtering out of the troubled state often reported more than one incident of insurgency. This made life difficult for the headline writers; they had a tough time choosing the point to highlight. A case in point is the news story that gave details of an effort to burn a mosque and also the kidnapping of a university professor. The headline writer made a valiant effort to put both the points in the headline, but could do justice to neither. The reader did not learn which mosque was the target of militant attack, nor who was abducted or from where.

Bid to burn
mosque, don
abducted

Another headline that left much to be desired was the one that spoke about the tax dues of Big Bull Harshad Mehta, when he was still alive. The headline writer abbreviated both income tax and wealth tax, though the second abbreviation is used as the acronym for ticketless travellers in India.

Harshad remains
top I-T, W-T
defaulter

Another headline that went haywire because of overloading was about Andhra Pradesh education officials who had fudged figures. The exercise was aimed to prove that Andhra Pradesh was more literate than Kerala, though this was factually incorrect. The headline writer decided to put both these points in the headline. The result was not very pleasing. The meaning got blurred and the headline became too long.

Headline used: **Education officials fudge 'records' to surpass Kerala's; 20 lakh children 'missing'**

Corrected headline: **AP officials tamper records; make state 'more literate' than Kerala**

RULE 21: MAKE SURE THAT THE NOUN AGREES WITH THE VERB IN NUMBER

Ask any headline writer and he/she will confirm that verbs have an amazing way of not agreeing with nouns in number. However, it is rare when one comes across a headline where both singular and plural forms of a verb have been used with the same subject.

One such headline was used when India beat South Korea in an exciting Asia Cup hockey semi-final match in Kuala Lumpur. This was inexcusable since the mistake was too obvious.

Headline used: **India** stun **South Korea,** enters **Asia Cup final**

Corrected Headline: **India** stuns **South Korea,** enters **Asia Cup final**

Another headline that was a victim of the same mistake was the one that related to the arrival of the Australian cricket team. The stand-in Australian captain Adam Gilchrist refused to speak to the press, saying that a press conference was scheduled for the following day. The headline writer joined the two points to make the headline look more attractive. But in the process an error was introduced.

Aussie team arrives **in India,** refuse **to speak to media**

The mistake was quite glaring. The singular and plural forms of verbs could not have been used for the same subject. Since team is singular, both the verbs should have been singular in number.

Aussie team arrives **in India,** refuses **to speak to media**

RULE 22: USE INDIAN TERMS

Headlines should use terms that are familiar to the ordinary Indian reader. A major problem today is the use of western metrics in headlines. Figures are given in millions, billions and even trillions. Barring a few Indians, the majority have a tough time translating these figures into the more familiar lakhs and crores.

A similar problem is the increasing use of dollars where too the American influence is becoming more visible. Takeover sums are given in dollars as also per capita incomes. A reader needs to mentally convert the dollars into Indian rupees to understand the import of a sale.

For instance, when eBay announced the takeover of India's top online auction firm Baazee.com, the newspapers headlined the story as:

eBay buys out Baazee for $50 million

However, they did not stop to ask themselves as to how much $50 million was in Indian rupees. This task was left to the readers. Was this right?

The thumb rule for any good headline is to keep it simple and easy to understand for every reader.

Rule 23: Rules for New Pacts and Treaties

Bilateral and multilateral agreements signed between governments are a major challenge for headline writers. The full form of the agreement is too long to be accommodated in the headline, and the acronym is too new to be known commonly.

A good example is the Joint Working Group that was set up by India and Turkey to combat terrorism during Prime Minister Atal Behari Vajpayee's visit to Turkey in 2003. Headline writers shortened the term Joint Working Group to JWG though it is doubtful that anyone outside the Prime Minister's party would have understood what JWG stood for.

Acronyms like JWG suffer from another problem. They are incomplete when used on their own. The following headline run by the Chennai edition of the *New Indian Express* on that day brought out this inconsistency:

**JWG with Turkey to
combat terrorism**

The headline writer should have realized that Indian and Turkish mandarins had coined the term Joint Working Group to refer to a team that would jointly monitor terrorism. The expansion of the term JWG would have cleared the air though the absence of the verb would still have crippled the headline. Also, the headline would have become too long for use once the acronym JWG was expanded.

**Joint Working Group with Turkey
to combat terrorism**

The first thing that the headline writer needed to do was to include a verb. This would have made the headline less opaque.

**India, Turkey to set up JWG
to combat terrorism**

or

**India, Turkey ink JWG pact
to combat terrorism**

The headline writer should have then tried to get around the acronym JWG. The reader would have understood the main news point if the headline was rewritten as:

**India, Turkey ink pact to
combat terrorism**

or

**India, Turkey to set up group
to combat terrorism**

RULE 24: USE OF PREPOSITIONS

A large number of headline errors result from the wrong use of prepositions. These errors can be categorized in two clear categories:

Where Meaning Changes

American actor Tom Cruise provided a great punning opportunity to headline writers when he rushed into a makeshift ladies toilet in a circus. However, one headline writer blew up the opportunity by choosing the wrong preposition.

Headline used: **Tom 'Cruises' in the ladies loo**
Corrected headline: **Tom 'Cruises' to the ladies loo**

The first headline implied that Tom Cruise went swishing around the ladies washroom. This was most unfair to the talented actor. All that he had done was to rush to the nearest washroom to relieve himself.

Where the Wrong Preposition is Used

Few Indians can lay claim to know the finer nuances of idiomatic English. Prepositional phrases, in particular, are a constant irritant. They flummox headline writers who are in search *of/for* the right words, are adverse *to/against* making mistakes, or would like to conform *to/with* style rules. The best is to refer to a dictionary whenever in doubt about a prepositional phrase.

RULE 25: FACTS AND GRAMMAR

Two headline errors that cannot be excused are factual and grammatical. The headline writers must learn that the best headline is the accurate headline. They cannot afford to make embarrassing slips about names and figures.

Injuries should not be turned into deaths and vice versa in accident stories. Similarly, Imphal should not become Agartala and July should not become August. The headline writers cannot hide behind the excuse that the figure or name was incorrect in the story. The mistake looks really ugly when played up in 36 or 48 points.

Grammatical errors are even more embarrassing. They reflect poorly on the skills of the copy desk. These errors may be classified in two categories.

Carelessness

This occurs when headline writers do not apply themselves to the task before them, but write the first headline that comes to their mind. When rain forced play to be called off in the Trentbridge Test between India and England, the headline writer chose to drop the preposition 'to' in an effort to fit the headline in three columns.

Shower forces umpires call of play

Another headline that caused merriment was the one that was related to portfolio assignment. It turned Ajit Singh into Food instead of the Food Minister of India. Once again the mistake occurred because the headline writer ran out of space to accommodate the word minister.

Scindia made HRD
Minister, Ajit Food

Ignorance

Everyone knows that the word heavens in the usage for heaven's sake has an apostrophe. So what does one say about this mistake in the *Asian Age*? (Fig. 7.18):

Original: **A film on Lalu: but for** heavens **sake why?**
Revised: **A film on Lalu: but for** heaven's **sake why?**

Fig. 7.18: *A usage error in a headline used in the* Asian Age.

8 | THE INTERNET HEADLINE

The danger of good stories going unread on the Internet because of weak headlines is too real. Internet readers have a wide choice, and can move from one site to another at the click of a mouse. The fact that they pay for every minute that they are online makes them even choosier about the stories they want to read.

They have only one path to reach a news report and that is the headline. This is in sharp contrast to a newspaper where the news report is run underneath a headline. Readers can scan the story even if the headline is run of the mill. This is not to say that the print media has the licence to write bland headlines; rather, it is to point out the physical possibility of a news report being read despite a poor headline.

FUNCTIONS

The primary function of an Internet headline is to encourage the reader to open a news report. Good headlines can spark reader interest and encourage them to click on the headline link, while dull and drab headlines may turn them off. That is why Internet headlines are called virtual gateways.

Some websites use teaser paragraphs to strengthen the headline. This is not a bad ploy because the reader can use the extra information to make the decision. But teaser paragraphs take space, and reduce the number of stories that can be showcased on a single screen.

Chhattisgarh worries over lack of raw material
RAIPUR: Until about a year ago, Chhattisgarh was concerned about how to woo investors in steel. A new worry is now plaguing the...<u>Full Story</u>

Tourist season yet to pick up in Himachal
SHIMLA: The long weekend and rising temperatures have failed to get tourists to the cool resorts of Himachal Pradesh....<u>Full Story</u>

Fig. 8.1: *Teaser paragraphs used to supplement information in headlines on* Newindpress.com

Most news sites therefore prefer to run teaser paragraphs with the most important stories of the day. The remaining headlines are hosted without any supporting text.

The Internet headlines are also used to provide contrast on the computer screen. But this function has a limited utility because the only way to provide contrast is to host headlines in colour. Use of large display types or bold and ornamental typefaces reduce the visual appeal of a page.

It is important to note that Internet headlines are not used to establish the news value of a story, which is a major function of print headlines. This is because a standard point size is used to display all headlines on the home page. The reader has no visual yardstick to establish the importance of a headline based on differing font sizes.

Similarly, all Internet headlines are spread across a uniform width. The user does not have the advantage of establishing news value of a report on the basis of headline width or the number of columns used to write a headline—as happens in the case of print headlines.

CHARACTERISTICS

The following are the most important attributes of an Internet headline.

Point Size

Internet headlines are written in a small point size. Generally, their point size is one or two points more than the body point size. Sometimes it is the same as used in the body text. But display types or large, ornamental fonts are not used. There are two reasons for this. One, a display type is too large and jarring to the eye given the size of the computer screen; and two, the small point size allows the Internet editor to use more words to write the headline. This is a big advantage because the editor can pack more information in the headline and make it more meaningful.

Colour

The majority of media sites use black fonts to write headlines because black stands out against a white background. The colour black is stark and appropriate for serious news reports.

In the early days of the Internet, the headlines, especially those that were used as hyperlinks, were in blue. This was the default colour that was generated by the programme when the text was hyperlinked. Today, it is possible to place hyperlinked text in any colour.

Font

It is important to choose the headline font carefully. The most popular Internet font is Arial. It is a sans serif font whose letters have a large x-height. This makes the font stand out on the computer screen. The two other fonts that are popularly used by media sites are Times New Roman and Verdana.

A news site that selects a font other than these three fonts is running a great risk. This is because these three fonts are universally available. The other fonts may or may not be available in a user system. When this happens the user will see junk characters on the computer screen.

KINDS OF HEADLINES

Media sites use two kinds of headlines on the home page. These are as follows:

Hyperlinked Headlines

The hyperlinked headlines are those where the hyperlink code is buried in the headline text. The user can click on these headlines to download the news report.

• Realism marks Musharraf's visit
• General's journey through war memories
• Flowers, not sword, for sake of peace
• Search on for next BJP leader
• Maoists drive away Indian survey team

Fig. 8.2: *Headlines used on the home page of* Newindpress.com *are not underlined. The user does not know if the text is hyperlinked or not till the cursor is moved over the text.*

Some websites underline the hyperlinked headlines. This is a useful tool because a reader realises that the headline is a link. The other websites avoid underlining to make the page look clean. In such cases, the user has to run the cursor over the headline to know if it is a link or not.

Fig. 8.3: Rediff.com *underlines the headlines so that the reader knows immediately if the text is a link or not. Also, Rediff uses bold fonts to highlight stories.*

Talks were positive: Musharraf
• **Pakistan thrash India	Score	Your say**
• **Musharraf to meet Vajpayee tomorrow**
• Kalam hosts lunch for Musharraf
• India, Pakistan to enhance trade
• **New train to Pakistan in December**

Plain text

Some media sites prefer to run the headlines as plain text, that is without hyperlinks. In these cases, the headline needs to be supported by a teaser paragraph that may carry the hyperlink.

No hyperlinks are used on the story page. Here the headlines function as titles only on top of the page. They are either placed flush left or centred, depending upon the style adopted by a media website.

WRITING THE INTERNET HEADLINE

The best Internet headlines are those that highlight the important points in the story effectively. They do not scrimp or scrounge on information but make full use of the fact that they have more words to write a headline.

The importance of extra information is borne out from the following headlines written on the re-enactment of the historic Dandi March in 2005.

Print: **The monotony of re-enactments**
Internet: **Dandi march enactment fails to enthuse Indians**

The first headline was written for print while the second headline was written for the Internet. Clearly, the second headline is more informative, and a better indicator of the tenor of the news report.

Another headline that gave extra information on the Internet was the one written for the wedding of Prince Charles with Camilla Parker Bowles.

Print: **Charles, Camilla tie the knot finally**
Internet: **Charles, Camilla tie the knot after 35-year long affair**

Internet headlines generally do not use shoulders or straplines to convey information. Also, Internet headlines need not be smart or pun on words. The following headlines would have worked brilliantly in print:

Three jeers for democracy	**Eat, blink and be merry**
True lies	**Bawdy builders**
Stable manners	**Lie for an aye**
Let the tough get going	**Futility in diversity**

However, they should not be used on the Internet. They would leave a reader mystified as to the subject of the story. In nine out of 10 cases, the reader would avoid clicking on such headlines.

The do's and don'ts that must be kept in mind while writing the Internet headline are more or less the same as those for writing the print headline (see Chapter 2).

These include use of simple and concrete words, building headlines around active verbs, avoiding the use of articles and auxiliary verbs, making sure that the majority of headlines carry proper attribution, use abbreviations sparingly, and reflect the tone and tenor of the story accurately.

CHAPTER HIGHLIGHTS

Functions of an Internet headline

1. Work as virtual gateways to news reports.

2. Spark reader interest.

3. Sometimes use colour to provide contrast.

Important characteristics

1. Written in a small point size.
2. Set in universally available fonts.
3. Mostly set in black; sometimes in colour.
4. Descriptive in nature.
5. Provide important information.

Kinds of headlines

1. Hyperlinked.

2. Sans links.

Print and Internet headlines: a comparison

Print headlines	Internet headlines
1. Use few words.	Use more words and provide more information.
2. Use display fonts.	Set in small points.
3. Can have multiple decks.	Written as a single deck.
4. Written on top of the story.	Work as links to stories also.
5. Establish news value of a story.	Play no such role.
6. Used to provide contrast on a page.	Can be used to provide contrast.
7. Use shoulders, straplines.	Avoid use of shoulders, straplines.

HEADLINE EXERCISE

Exercise 1

Go through a media website and locate ten headlines where the Internet Editor has used description to provide extra information in a headline.

Exercise 2

Write an Internet headline for the five news reports that follow using the given headline parameters.

Point size: 12
Case: Upper-lower
Number of letters: 56
Number of decks: One

News Report 1

TIRUNELVELI (ENS): A six-year-old girl suffered severe burns when she accidentally fell into a vessel containing hot sambhar at her school in Subramaniapuram, near Puliyangudi, in Tirunelveli district.

The incident, which occurred on Wednesday, came to light only on Friday after Vasudevanallur BDO Dharmaraj lodged a complaint with Puliyangudi police.

Police said Isakiammal, a standard II student and daughter of Murugan of Subramaniapuram, had joined the queue to get her noon meals when she slipped and fell into the vessel containing hot sambhar. She suffered serious burns and was rushed to the Tenkasi GH. The police have registered a case against three persons — noon meal organiser Devadoss, cook Chellammal and helper Lakshmi.

News Report 2

KOCHI (ENS): Feminists will have reason to cheer as in a virtual role reversal, it's the hitherto pampered male who's now doling out dowry for a bride.

For the growing money order economy fuelled by well-paid nurses working abroad and the fall in the number of women in the community have prompted Knanaya Christian families to do a U-turn in terms of offering dowry.

The Knanaya community is a Catholic sect now facing a unique demographic problem: an acute shortage of women. As a result the number of bachelors within the community is swelling by the day, so that the average age of an unmarried male in the community is 33. Desperation has resulted in the bridegroom's family offering dowry to the bride's family.

Church sources say that more than 90 per cent of the community's womenfolk in the age group of 20–45 years are either working as nurses or in the medical field across the globe, and they are raking in the moolah.

A natural fallout has been a rise in income levels of these women's families who have now upped the ante and seek alliances from affluent families or persons who can migrate to the country where the girl is working. As a result, men with low-paid jobs are bearing the brunt, unable to find life partners.

News Report 3

BANGALORE (ENS): Making a long list of household items to be bought from the nearby super market? Hold for a while, it might be a futile exercise as you would be welcomed there by empty shelves.

Manufacturing companies are still perplexed on VAT (value added tax) and have not released fresh stocks, say supermarket managers.

Several outlets of Food World including Sadashivnagar, Sanjaynagar and Nilgiris stores on Brigade, Jayanagar, Kammanhalli did not have sufficient products on their racks.

"Our shelves have shrunken. A majority of the manufacturing companies are not releasing fresh products and new price list," says a supermarket owner in Vasant-nagar.

Even fast moving and regularly used products like shaving sets, biscuits, beverages, energy drinks were out of stock from past one week, says Vanaja, manager of a super-market.

"I see consumers go from one shop to another in search of these items," she says.

A consumer adds: "The companies and the authorities should do something to end this crisis."

One of the supermarkets had reportedly called the companies and were told that stocks were being held back due to confusion over price fixation on the production following the implementation of VAT.

However, the companies promised to release fresh stocks in the next one week.

News Report 4

TIRUPATI (UNI): After a gap of eight years, All India Radio (AIR), Tirupati on Saturday broadcast the "Suprabatham" — the first hymn chanted in the Sri Venkateswara temple at Tirumala — from 0300 hrs to 0330 hrs on the happy occasion of Telugu New Year, "Ugadi."

New administrators, including Tirumala Tirupati Devasthanam (TTD) executive officer A P V N Sarma and special officer, A V Dharma Reddy took efforts for the broadcast of religious programmes from Saturday. The broadcast could be heard over a radius of 150 km from Tirupati.

Apart from "Suprabatham" and "Vedaparayanam" in the morning and "Sahasradee-palankara" in the evening, AIR also broadcast feature songs on lord Venkateswara, by saint-poets like Annamacharya.

There would be six hours of programmes a day by TTD, UNI was told.

AIR, Tirupati, was charging an amount of Rs 500 per hour for the broadcast. The customary charge was Rs 5,000 per hour.

News Report 5

MAHBOOBNAGAR/KURNOOL (ENS): Search operations in Nallamala forests by the Grey Hounds personnel of the elite anti-naxal wing have been intensified after the Maoists' vain bid to attack Dindi police station in Nalgonda district on Thursday night.

Security has been beefed up at all police stations adjoining the Nallamala forests in view of the bandh call given by the Maoists in Nalgonda and Mahboobnagar districts to protest against the killing of their leaders G Srisailam and his wife Venkatamma in an encounter last week.

The bandh, of course, passed off peacefully in the naxal-affected areas with commercial establishments including shops remaining closed. The APSRTC suspended its services to interior places fearing attack from the extremists.

According to reports, a courier of the CPI (Maoist) informed a private news channel on Friday that the Grey Hounds personnel moved into the forests on a tip off that top Maoist leaders including party's state secretary Ramakrishna were holding a meeting.

The police, however, denied the reports of encircling Ramakrishna's hide-out. "It was a routine operation and nothing else," Prakasam district superintendent of police Mahesh Chandra Ladda told this newspaper from Ongole.

However, former emissaries of the CPI (Maoist) Vara Vara Rao and Kalyana Rao demanded that the combing operations should be stopped immediately. Balladeer Gaddar also faxed a message to Governor S K Shinde seeking his intervention to stop the search operations.

According to an ENS report from Kurnool, the police and Jana Shakti Naxalites exchanged fire for about half an hour at Utla village near Ahobilam on Friday morning. No one was injured in the incident and the police recovered 38 kit bags indicating that some top leaders had held a meeting with their cadres.

Glossary

Anchor: A soft story used at the base of the first page. The headline of such a story is different from headlines used for hard news stories. It is more creative and eye-catching.

Banner: A headline that is run across all eight columns on top of the front page. The banner is used for momentous events and is set in big and bold letters. It is also referred to as Streamer in the US.

Bold typeface: A typeface that is set in a distinguishing bold and black tone.

Box headline: A headline written for a news story that is placed in the belly of a main story. The term derives its name from the fact that the related story is placed in a ruled box.

Bumped headline: It is an American term used to indicate two headlines of the same point size and the same width run side by side on a page. Its British equivalent is Tombstone.

Deck: A single line of headline type.

Display type: A general term used to refer to the type that is set in a much larger point size than the body text.

Downstyle: It is the system of capitalization where the first letter of a headline and the first letter of proper nouns used in it are placed in capitals.

em: A term used to measure the length of a line of type during the hot metal era. Technically, em is the area occupied by the square of a letter. Em was so called because the capital letter M in any typeface is almost as wide as it is high.

en: En was another measurement term used during the hot metal era. An en was equal to half of em because the square of letter en is half of the square of letter em. However, both ems and ens have fallen into disuse today and typographers prefer to express lengths in picas.

Font: Font is a full set of characters/letters available in a specific weight/style in a family. It includes all alphabets, numerals and punctuation marks both in capitals and upper-lower case.

Headline: The title of a news report run in display type to catch the attention of the readers. A headline summarizes the most important point in a news report.

Headline width: The number of columns across which a headline runs.

Headline weight: The weight of a typeface depends on its blackness. The one that is blacker is said to have a heavier weight

Italics: These are gently sloping letters with or without serifs. They may have thick and thin stems or uniform stems, but their distinguishing characteristic remains their slanted letters. Newspapers set headlines in italics to display a light or a non-serious story. The credit of developing the italics type face goes to Aldus Manutius.

Kern: The condensation or expansion of space between characters that go to make a word. It can also be defined as the horizontal scaling of text.

Kicker: The headline that is written on top of the main headline. It is set in a point size that is less than the point size used for the main headline. It was initially used to indicate the subject of a news story but now it is used to highlight news points not covered in the main headline. Kicker is an American term and is gradually replacing shoulder, which is a British term, in Indian newspapers.

Leading: The term used to designate the space between two typeset lines. Another term from the hot metal era, it owes its origin to the thin strips of lead that were used to separate lines of type.

Multiple Decks: When the headline runs across two or three lines — or even more — then it is said to have been set in multiple decks.

Pica: It is a unit used to measure lengths. A pica is made of twelve points, which on the metric scale is equal to one-sixth of an inch or 0.1666 inches. Pica today is the most popular term used for measuring lengths.

Useful pica metrics: 12 points = 1 pica or 1/16" (0.166"), and 6 picas = 1" (or 0.996").

Point: It is a measurement unit used to indicate type sizes. The point system was designed by Pierre Fournier in 1837 and which, with slight modifications, continues even today. One point is equal to 1/72 of an inch or 0.0138 inches.

Point size: It is the height of a typeface.

Reverse: A typesetting style where the letters are white and the background is grey or black. Today, it is possible to compose letters in a wide variety of colours; similarly, the background colours can be changed to make the type stand out.

Reverse shoulder: A headline written beneath the main headline. It is written in a point size that is smaller than the one used to write the main headline, and is generally used to highlight a new point. It can also be used to amplify the main headline. The term strapline is replacing reverse shoulder in several Indian newspapers.

Roman: They are upright letters with thick and thin stems and small, line strokes known as serifs. The credit of developing Roman letters goes to a Frenchman Nicholas Jenson who developed them while working in Italy in the fifteenth century.

Shoulder: The headline that is written on top of the main headline. It is set in a point size that is smaller than the one used for the main headline. It was initially used to indicate the subject of a news story but now it is used to highlight news points not covered in the main headline. The term kicker is replacing shoulder in several Indian news-papers.

Standing heads: The headlines that are not changed every day. They are used to headline regular items like the weather, city diary, etc., and are also known as stet heads.

Strapline: A headline written beneath the main headline. It is written in a point size that is smaller than the point size used to write the main headline, and is generally used to highlight a new point. It can also be used to amplify the main headline. It is an American term, and is replacing the British term reverse shoulder, in Indian newspapers.

Streamer: A headline that is run across all eight columns on top of the page. The streamer is used for momentous events and is set in big and bold letters. This too is an American term and is becoming more popular than Banner in India.

Subhead: A one or two-word headline inserted at the head of a paragraph to break the monotony of a solid column of type. It is also written as a headline for items that are stringed together as a necklace like city briefs. Sub-heads are generally written in bold letters in the same point size as the body text.

Tombstone: When two headlines of the same point size and the same width are run side by side on a page. A tombstone is also called a bumped headline in the American press.

Sans Serifs: The typefaces whose individual stroke is of the same width and does not end with any tiny, decorative stroke. Their stark and barren character makes them most suitable for writing headlines.

Serifs: The type faces that use decorative flourishes at the end of main strokes to lend elegance to the character.

Index

Anchor, 26

Banner, 34, 35
Bumped headline, 40

Crossheads, 124

Definition of a headline, 17
Display feature headlines, 141–44; graphics as props, 144; illustrations as props, 143; photographs as props, 142; varying typefaces, 141
Decks, 48
Do's and don'ts of headlines, 169–96; avoid auxiliary verbs, 177; avoid confusing constructions, 173; avoid modifiers, 170; avoid overloading, 192; avoid repetition of words, 174; be careful with sobriquets, 180; do not use articles, 178; do not imply meanings, 174; each deck as a unit, 183; facts and grammar, 196; how to use attribution, 181; malapropisms, 173; new pacts and treaties, 194–95; noun, verb and number, 193; place verbs ahead of nouns, 176; select words carefully, 171; use abbreviations carefully, 179; use concrete words, 169; use of adjectival phrase, 184; use of apostrophes, 191; use of prepositions, 195; use of prepositional phrase, 185; use of punctuation marks, 187–90; use of verb phrase, 184; use present tense, 186; use simple and short words, 169; use verbs, 175; visually pleasing headlines, 182
Downstyle, 36

Feature headline tips, 144; creative use of verbs, 152; play on acronyms, 146; play on book titles, 147; play on film titles, 148; play on names, 146; play on phonetics, 149; play on proverbs/sayings, 150; play on radio/TV jingles 149; play on themes/images, 152; play on words, 144
Font, 37
Functions of a headline, 24–33; depict mood, 30; establish news value, 24; give identity, 32; index the news, 24; provide typographical relief, 31; set the tone, 31

Headline count, 50

Internet headline, 197–201; characteristics, 198; hyperlinked heads, 199; functions, 197
Italics 29, 37

Kerning, 37
Kicker, 38, 119
Kinds of headlines, cause and effect, 65; commentative headlines, 68; descriptive headlines, 59; editorial headlines, 101–02; feature headlines, 138–53, figurative headlines, 66; hinglish headlines, 71; letters headlines, 102; magazine headlines, 153; multiple point, 61; number headlines, 98–100; question headlines, 95–98; quotes as headline, 89–94; running story, 62; sidebars, 73; surprise headlines, 71
Keywords, 48

Navigation heads, 126–27

Point size, 27, 39

Quotes as headline, 89–94; editing of quotes, 93–94; partial quotes, 94; use of attribution, 90–94

Read in headlines, 121–22
Reverse, 39

Reverse shoulder, 122–24
Roman letters, 29, 40

Sans serif, 41
Serif, 41
Shoulder, 38, 119
Sidehead, 124–26
Standing heads, 40, 127
Stet heads, 40, 127
Strapline, 122–24
Style, 29

Subhead, 40

Tombstone, 40
Traditional feature heads, 139–41

Use of punctuation marks, 187–91; full stop,
187; comma, 188; colons, 189; long dash/
hyphen, 190; quotation marks, 191

Weight, 28, 37
Width, 25, 37

About the Author

Sunil Saxena is Vice President (Content and Services), Express Network Private Limited, Chennai, which is the Internet company of the New Indian Express Group, a leading Indian media house. He has 28 years of experience as a print and Internet journalist and as a teacher of journalism. He has worked for the *Times of India*, *India Today*, the *Business India* Group and the *Pioneer*. He was the first Dean of the Asian College of Journalism which was set up by the B.D. Goenka Foundation in Bangalore in 1994.